Put That Light Out

ILKESTON AT WAR 1939-1941

Garnet Langton

Published by Garnet Langton
P.O. Box 4, Bournemouth, BH1 1YL
E-mail: garnet@theoffice.net
Web page: http://www.theoffice.net/garnet
Copyright Garnet Langton 1997
ISBN 0 9527 05214

Printed by How's Business Ltd.,
Dalkeith Hall, Dalkeith Steps, Bournemouth, BH1 1YL

2

Contents

Illustrations and cover design by
CHRIS LANGTON
E-mail: studiocl@bournemouth-net.co.uk

For PAT

Acknowledgements

I would like to thank Nigel Overton, curator of the Erewash Museum for permission to reproduce the Spitfire and Tobacco Fund vouchers; Mike Jobling and his helpful staff at Ilkeston Local Studies Library for their valued co-operation during my researches; and to Jeff Hallam and Cyril Charlton for their wartime reminiscences.

Also by Garnet Langton:
Third In The Wheelbarrow Race

CHAPTER ONE
THE UMBRELLA MAN

The first talk of war I remember was in 1938 when Dad came home with a new record to play on our wind-up gramophone. It was called 'The Umbrella Man' and went:

Toodle lum-a lum-a, toodle lum-a lum-a, toodle hi-ay,

Any umbrellas, any umbrellas, to fix today,

Bring your parasol, it may be small, it may be big,

He repairs them all with what you call, a thinga-ma-jig.

Naturally, I was curious to know who this man was who wanted to mend our umbrellas and go on his way. Dad told me he was Neville Chamberlain, the Prime Minister. I had seen pictures of him carrying an umbrella, looking very old fashioned in a wing collar similar to the one my old Sunday School teacher wore. He had a grey moustache and prominent teeth and in one picture I saw on the front of Dad's Daily Herald he was waving a piece of paper.

'He's trying to stop a war breaking out with Germany' I was told. 'He's just been to see Hitler at Munich and now we should have peace - so they say.'

Dad had fought in the first world war. After joining up at eighteen he served in France where he was wounded in the right hand in 1918, almost at the end of the war, and was discharged the following January. My younger brother, sister and I used to look at his hand: you could still see the scar where the bullet went through.

'We hope there's not going to be another war' were my parent's sentiments. People remembered the Spanish Civil War, a couple of years previously when cities were devastated by bombing and thousands of civilians were killed. They knew that if another war came, it wouldn't be like the First World War which was fought out in France by the military.

'Next time it'll be bombing and poison gas.'

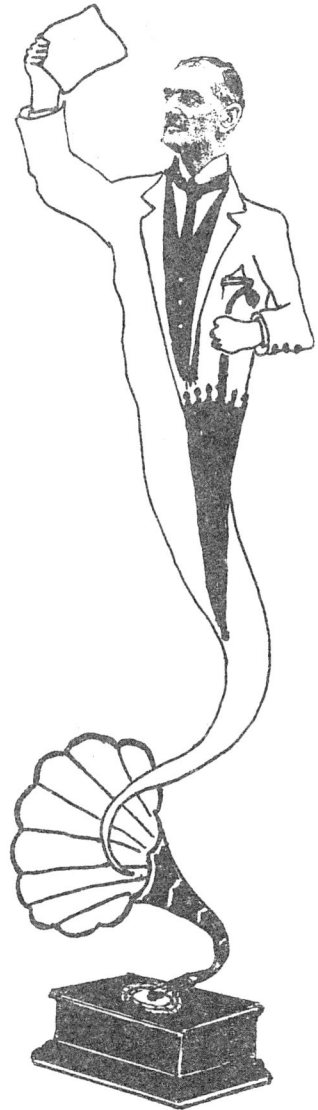

5

So was it going to be 'peace in our time' as the papers were saying? Nobody seemed to be really sure in spite of the umbrella man's piece of paper. At Munich, Hitler had persuaded him to force Czechoslovakia to give up part of her territory, the Sudetenland. I had looked at my atlas and found Czechoslovakia right in the middle of Europe bordering on Germany, Austria, Hungary and Poland. In March 1939 Germany suddenly occupied the rest of Czechoslovakia and everybody said that meant trouble.

'We're not ready for a war' was my Uncle Billy's considered opinion. Uncle Billy always kept up with the news, reading his Daily Sketch from cover to cover every weekday and the Sunday Pictorial on Sunday. Whatever had happened, was happening or likely to happen, Uncle Billy knew. He did tell me that we were starting to build more planes, tanks and guns and said the army planned to have 32 divisions: they only had couple of divisions for overseas at that time and the RAF had only six squadrons of first rate fighters. And then, of course, there was the ARP.

Air raid precautions had started in 1938 when the country had been divided into twelve Civil Defence regions, then into districts right down to borough level. In January 1939 a 48 page handbook entitled NATIONAL SERVICE thudded through our letter box. On the second page was a message from Chamberlain himself.

'To secure peace we must be strong,' it said. ' The country needs your services and you are anxious to play your part' which might sound a bit presumptuous today, but it didn't in 1939. 'This guide will point the way. I ask you to read it carefully and to decide how you can help.'

Dad was studying it closely, dismissing the first part 'mainly for younger men' as he was over 40 and didn't really fit into the armed forces, either as a regular or a reserve, nor could he see himself joining the police, fire brigade or one of the nursing services. The second part of the booklet 'mainly for older men' was for those over 30 who were urged to become air raid wardens, ambulance drivers, special constables, territorials in anti-aircraft units or balloon squadrons, clerks, or members of first aid parties, decontamination squads or the Observer Corps.

'Physically fit' men between the ages of 25 and 50 were wanted for Rescue and Demolition Parties, especially those used to handling jacks, tackle and scaffolding and 'educated' men over 45 and women over 18 who were capable of taking down telephone messages were required for report centres and communications. Many people fought shy of using the telephone in fact few households had phones. The only time some people used a phone was to call the doctor in an emergency and even then a neighbour or local shopkeeper was asked to do the phoning.

As Dad studied the National Service handbook, Mum called out: 'You've got enough on your plate without joining any of them. You're already working all hours God sends.'

This was largely true. Dad was in full time work in the artificial silk processing plant at British Celanese working a shift system of six days and occasionally working his day off. The years of chronic unemployment had receded. The thirties had seen depressed areas, hunger marches, the Means Test, bad housing and far too many people existing on bread and marge and cups of tea.

Britain was a country of heavy industry: coalmines, shipyards and iron and steel works. My home town of Ilkeston was a working class town with thousands employed in the mines, iron and concrete manufacture and textile and hosiery factories. The threat of war had resulted in a demand for more goods including weapons: guns, tanks, planes and warships.

War clouds may have been gathering at the beginning of 1939 but the Langtons were thinking how much life had improved during the past year: full time employment, more money and a new semi-detached house rented for fifteen shillings a week. Some people were even able to afford a car: there were almost two millions of them on the roads in 1939, one for every 24 persons. One of the boys in my class at Granby Boys' School had been seen in a car, apparently his father's, and we silently envied him.

But my father too was becoming more affluent and we realised he was beginning to think of spending some of it when he began saying that the old wind-up gramophone was on its last legs.

'Won't last much longer,' he remarked on several occasions, although it seemed just the same to me. This was followed by visits to each of the wireless stores in the town. We knew something was in the offing.

Then one day the dramatic announcement was made. 'I'm buying a new electric radiogram and it's a beauty, look at this' he said producing a copy of the Daily Herald with a large advert from the London furnishers Barkers. The illustration certainly looked impressive with its imposing wooden cabinet.

'Can you afford it?' enquired Mum taken aback by such an expensive purchase, twelve guineas I believe.

'Of course I can afford it. I wouldn't have sent for it if I'd not got the money' he retorted rather testily.

Dad liked buying by post, often seduced by tempting adverts in newspapers and magazines: that's how I acquired the Daily Express World Atlas and Gazetteer, Odham's Complete Self Educator and These Tremendous Years (de luxe edition) and several other Readers' Offers.

Excitement built up over the next few days while we awaited the arrival of the radiogram. I found myself hurrying home from school each day for an early inspection ('has it come yet?'). The day it arrived I came home to find Dad opening up the packing case in which it had arrived, well protected by straw and corrugated cardboard. The packing was removed to reveal the handsome polished walnut case standing about two feet in height and about the same length. With the help of my mother it was manoeuvred into position in the front room of the house, the room we used on Saturdays and Sundays or when we had special guests.

All the family - my parents, sister, brother and myself - stood back in admiration, the rich brown cabinet reflecting the afternoon sunlight dancing through the net curtains. Elegant, beautiful, lovely and smashing were some of the adjectives used to describe our new acquisition.

'A nice piece of furniture as well' added my mother who enthusiastically joined in the praise, her original scepticism forgotten. She knew it was sending out a message: the Langtons now possessed a quality item from a top London store. We had arrived.

Dad connected it up (my offer to help was spurned) and we sat and listened, first to the radio, taking in Midland Regional, Northern Regional, Radio Luxembourg, Radio Normandy, Hilversum and a host of other stations which were new to us. But it was the records we wanted to listen to so Dad, sensing our impatience, switched to 'Gram' and off we went tapping our feet to the rousing Sousa marches Blaze Away and Washington Greys. Then came the Umbrella Man (of course) before it was Mum's turn to hear her favourites: The Lord's My Shepherd (Crimond) and Jesus Shall Reign Where're The Sun (Rimmington).

There was a smile on Dad's face as he produced the next record, carefully removing it from its new paper cover. 'And here's one you haven't heard yet.'

'What is it?' Three children's voices spoke in unison. He was still smiling as the record started to play. After the first couple of bars Mum called out 'Lambeth Walk!' Jumping to her feet she began to dance around the room singing:

Any time you're Lambeth Way,

Any evening, any day,

You'll find us all doin' the Lambeth Walk,

Everything's free and easy,

Do as you darn well pleasey....

By this time we were all on our feet dancing to the rolling tempo which had taken the country by storm. If there had been a Top Ten then, it would easily have been number one. Although Lambeth Walk was just a street in a working class area of east London, we read in the paper that the song had become popular all over Europe. They were playing it in Paris restaurants and even in Czechoslovakia which was in crisis. Now we could play it whenever we liked along with our other favourites and the promise of more to come. The new radiogram had brought an extra dimension to our lives.

'Beautiful, beautiful tone' said Dad and we all nodded in agreement.

Then came the inevitable instructions. My sister and brother were ordered not to touch it, nor even get near it. 'Keep well away, no toys or games round here' my mother said. However, I was honoured and was shown how to switch it on, turn up the volume, find a station and switch off ('but always turn the volume down before you switch it off'). I was warned however to leave the record player alone. 'I'll play the records so don't you meddle with it' ordered Dad.

Keeping the cabinet 'nice' was a matter of concern and polishing it became something of a ritual. Each weekend the Mansion Polish was liberally applied followed by buffing with a soft cloth. Disaster struck some months later when a scratch appeared on the top but an inquest failed to find the culprit, so we were all admonished and threatened.

Uncle Arthur was brought in to inspect the damage. He was one of my mother's older brothers and an expert french polisher, a trade he had learned from his father who had been a furniture maker and dealer in Ilkeston's main street, Bath Street, in the early 1900s.

Arthur arrived with the tools of his trade, turpentine, glass cloths, polishes and rags and set about the task of removing the offending scratch. I was watching him from a distance but was eventually driven out of the room by the overpowering smell of turps and polish while he diligently continued working on the damaged area. He had a break at one stage for a snack but by the end of the day it was finished, the eyesore had been removed and it was back to its near pristine condition.

'How much do we owe you?' asked Mum, knowing that he wouldn't charge.

'Oh no, that's all right, it's nothing!' came the reply. This was typical of Arthur, a fine french polisher who never really made a success of the business as he seldom charged relations and friends and was too easy-going with paying customers. Much of the time I knew him he had labouring or menial jobs where he was sure of a wage, rather than pursuing his craft.

He was also a competent artist producing pen and ink and pencil sketches, mainly of the locality, but he never tried to sell them, many were given away. Some of the sketches were reproduced in a local newspaper, again without fee. His life ended in a tiny alms house filled with his sketches, books, diaries and an organ which he played regularly.

The first six months of 1939 brought many changes. Wardens' Posts and First Aid Posts started to appear in the town, some in houses, some in schools and other buildings, each one manned by five or six wardens. There was supposed to be one post to every 400 to 500 inhabitants, each one heavily sandbagged. The job of the wardens in the event of war was to patrol the area and report any incidents during an air raid. Incidents could mean anything from large scale bombing, unexploded bombs and incendiaries down to minor security matters. It was then the warden's duty to call stretcher parties, rescue units, fire brigade, police, mobile canteen or whatever was appropriate and then make a report.

The reports were co-ordinated at a central headquarters, in Ilkeston's case at Manor House in Manor Road. A system of colour codes was used to inform ARP units of the severity of any activity. Yellow was a preliminary warning that enemy aircraft were in the Midlands, purple meant that they were heading our way, red indicated they were in our vicinity when the siren on the top of the Town Hall was sounded. All available ARP personnel would then have been brought in and we should have to take cover either in shelters or protected rooms in our own homes.

For weeks we had watched Corporation workmen filling sandbags and placing them against our schools to protect them against bomb blast. Passing Bennerley Schools each day I saw the pile of sandbags creeping up the building, obscuring windows and doors, and at Granby Boys' which I attended in the summer of 1939 the same thing was happening. The classrooms became darker and we had to have the lights on. Other schools were receiving the same treatment as well as the library, town hall, police station and wardens' posts. I heard that Cavendish School was a full scale First Aid Post with stretchers, ambulances and full-time qualified staff.

Wardens in their dark uniforms and tin hats were stalking round the town, but they were not popular. Peering into one of the Wardens Posts one day on our way home from school, a friend and I saw four of them sitting at a table playing cards, smoking cigarettes and drinking tea. On seeing us, one of the wardens leapt up and unceremoniously bundled us out of the entrance with dire threats as to what would happen if he caught us again.

'Who does he think he is?' demanded my pal. 'I know him, he lives down our street, my dad says he's a big head'.

When I told my father his reply was: 'Give 'em a uniform and a tin hat and they act like little Hitlers. Some of them are getting paid £3 a week for that, for doing nowt except play cards and order us about. Even part-timers get their wages made up. It's a scandal.' I am reminded of this every time I watch the television series Dad's Army and the officious warden Hodges.

Special constables too were not always popular. A cartoon in the London Evening Standard at the time showed two gossiping women eyeing a special with one saying 'He used to be such a nice mild little man but now he's a proper Gestapo.' However, there was a serious side to it and the public were being made aware how to deal with emergencies in case of air attacks. ARP displays were put on by local groups in Ilkeston on how to put out an incendiary with a stirrup pump - some households were being issued with them - and we also saw how decontamination squads worked in the event of gas attacks and how to deal with air raid casualties.

On our way to school we also saw trenches being dug in Granby Park (air raid shelters were always called trenches then). A dozen or more perspiring men wielding picks and shovels, others pushing wheelbarrows, were digging out earth. Pre-cast concrete sections were piled up nearby ready to be put into position. These were the days before JCBs and mechanical diggers! It all looked very hard work underlining what Dad had advised me: get an office job, not a labourer's.

One of the most significant reminders of approaching war was the issue of gas masks. By the summer of 1939 we all had them. I have a recollection of collecting and trying mine on at Bennerley ARP post and being instructed by a warden to hold the mask by the straps, stick out chin and insert the face. Of course it didn't fit so there was a lot of adjusting of straps before a good fit was achieved. The first thing I noticed was the lingering smell of rubber. After wearing it for a time the eye piece would steam up, just like a window in a hot room after rain.

There was a poster telling us what to do in case of a gas attack. If we heard the gas rattles which were the warning signals we were to hold our breaths, put on our masks and close any windows if we were at home. If we were out of doors we were to take off our hats (nearly everybody wore hats then), put on our masks, turn up our collars, then put our hands in our pockets.

The poster went on to inform us: If you get gassed keep your gas mask on even if you feel discomfort. If discomfort continues go to the First Aid Post. If there was liquid or blister gas, we were to dab, not rub, the splash with a handkerchief which should then be destroyed. 'No.2 Ointment' should then be rubbed well into place, apparently available at sixpence a jar from any chemist. Failing this we were to wash the affected parts with soap and water.

As kids, we thought the gas masks were fun and experimented by blowing into them, making rude noises, but adults, especially the elderly, were protesting and finding them very uncomfortable, even when they were properly fitted.

My grandmother had tried hers once, hated the smell, said she couldn't hear properly in it and concluded 'I'd rather be gassed than wear it.'

Each householder was being urged to create a gas-proof room in his house. This involved sealing up cracks, doors and windows with special sealing tape or putty and I recollect several hours spent in the front room - which Dad had decided was our best refuge - fixing tape. As we had no putty we used newspapers soaked in a bucket of water until they became a pulp. It sounds so primitive now but at the time it was a deadly serious business.

A blackout exercise took place on the night of 10/11 August to remind us of the imminence of war. Every household was told to have blackout curtains in place. My mother had been measuring the windows in the house, calculating the amount of material required which had to be thick enough to prevent any light showing outside. There had been a rush to drapers' shops to buy sufficient material before stocks ran out. The house had been a hive of activity measuring, cutting, machining and fitting curtains.

Even so the only rooms blacked out at first were the kitchen where we spent our evenings, my parent's bedroom and the bathroom. Dad solved this temporary problem by removing the light bulbs in the unprotected rooms, so at the beginning of the war we went to bed with candles, just like a Victorian pastiche.

My mother decided our first blackout curtains were not thick enough and blamed herself for not buying thicker material, so more curtaining had to be bought ('this is costing me a fortune') and those she had already made were turned into double thickness.

Neighbours were also making inspections of their own and other people's blackout arrangements.

'Can't afford proper curtains' said one pointing to sheets hanging in one window, 'and look at that, brown paper fixed wi' drawing pins. They'll soon get sick o' putting that up every night.'

On the other hand, some householders had been to a great deal of trouble. Some handymen had made shutters from material and wooden laths or pieces of wood, and artistic types had decorated their blackout material with designs and I remember seeing one with stars stitched on.

Then we had to reinforce the window panes to stop splintering of glass. There were a couple of ways of doing this, one was to apply netting to the panes, the other to stick on strips of gummed paper in a criss-cross pattern. The first method was preferred as there was less obstruction of light.

Wardens and policemen were patrolling the streets on the night of the exercise, advising and warning offenders. At first it was warnings but when war started the authorities got tough and many were fined.

At the beginning of August I was eleven and would soon be starting my new school, Hallcroft Boys, situated near the town centre. The school cap had been purchased and I was gearing myself up ready to go: lessons there would be much harder and would include French which sounded quite exciting if not a little daunting as well as woodwork and science which were new to me. However we were suddenly informed that owing to the national emergency the school would not be opening as planned in the first week of September as the air raid shelters had not been built. This was greeted with pleasure but not by our parents ('as if you don't get enough holidays in the summer').

Then we heard about evacuation. Children in big cities would be evacuated to country districts so what was going to happen in Ilkeston, a town of 35,000 with a large ironworks on our doorstep; would we be evacuated? Apparently not, in fact some of the outlying villages were getting ready to receive evacuees. Billeting officers had been round earlier in the year canvassing householders willing to take them.

During the last week of August we saw pictures of children in London where the schools had been opened up specially to marshal those waiting to be evacuated. The evacuation began on the Friday with hundreds of thousands of children boarding trains in London and the big cities including nearby Nottingham and Derby. They had labels round their necks, gas mask cases on string dangling from their shoulders and were carrying cases, bags and brown paper parcels with their clothes and rations. It was a voluntary scheme and in four days more than 1,300,000 were moved in 4,000 special trains.

On the same day as the evacuation started - Friday the first of September - we were listening to the six o'clock news - everybody was now tuned in to news bulletins - when the announcement came that National and Regional services were being merged and in future there would only be one programme. This seemed to bring home to everybody the seriousness of the situation.

The following day, a hot sunny one I remember, people were talking in groups on Cotmanhay Road as I performed my Saturday routine, running errands for my grandmother which earned a silver sixpence. There was also the opportunity to read Chips and Jester, penny comics which Uncle Billy

12

had delivered at Grandmas's house where he lived. He also took the Daily Sketch ('the picture paper') and John Bull magazine. But it was Chips which attracted me and Saturdays would not have been the same without catching up with the exploits of Wearie Willie and Tired Tim.

There was a sombre atmosphere in each shop I went in. Instead of talking about their holidays or what was happening at work or how Derbyshire had beaten Nottinghamshire by 147 runs in the cricket match on the Rutland ground earlier in the week, the talk was of Hitler, the invasion of Poland, war and the evacuation of children. Some families were worried about the call-up which had already begun, the elderly scared of air raids and gas attacks. Listening to them, it sounded as if the war had already started.

'I'll have an extra two pound of sugar and another packet of tea this week' said one old soul in front of me 'and give me a tin of Carnation milk, they'll all keep.'

'Yes, I'm stocking up an' all', chipped in a woman at the back of me. 'Once this war starts we'll be on rations.' That seemed to be the general sentiment on this sombre day. I knew that my own mother had been stocking up as I had seen packets of tea and sugar in the wardrobe.

Back home, the wireless was on with record programmes and Sandy Macpherson at the organ, frequently interrupted by news bulletins on the deteriorating situation. Parliament was in emergency session, the first regulations under the Emergency Powers (Defence) Act were being issued, the armed forces had been mobilised, liability for military service had been extended to include all fit men between the ages of 18 and 41, railway stations were packed with school children being evacuated from large towns and cities, and Hitler's troops were marching through Poland.

I went to the afternoon matinee at the Kings to catch up with the weekly episode of a cowboy film but even here the kids were talking about war.

'My dad says there's going to be a war and we might get bombed and gassed.'

'Our Spitfires and Hurricanes'll shoot 'em down.'

'Jerry's got Stuka dive bombers that come screaming down at you and then drops its bombs.'

'We've got guns at Dover that'll shoot 'em down before they get here.'

Even the cowboy film and the cartoons took second place to the war situation. That evening dark clouds began to gather in the sky after the heat of the day.

'We're going to have a thunderstorm' predicted my mother as she began putting the blackout curtains in place. She was right. As I went to bed with my candle I could see flashes in the sky which I thought may be guns but soon the rains came with thunder and lightning right overhead. Perhaps this was a portent of what was to come. None of us could be sure but this could be the last day of peace.

I woke next morning to find the storm had gone. It was a bright sunny day when I came downstairs. Breakfast was cooking and the wireless was on. Dad, who always got up early, even when it was his day off, had been listening to the seven o'clock news.

'No reply from Hitler. It looks like war' he said briefly, almost as if we had been waiting for a letter and the postman had passed us by.

I knew about the ultimatum to Hitler, everybody did. He had been given till eleven o'clock to withdraw his troops from Poland. My parents were all tensed up; I had never seen them quite like this and it worried me because they were worried. Dad went into the back garden and started to dig the trench which he had planned. He had been waiting to pick the last crop of peas and runner beans for the space. Now with sleeves rolled up on that sunny morning he was digging out the earth for our own air raid shelter. A couple of sheets of corrugated iron and several pieces of timber lay nearby.

'Perhaps I'll run a cable and put some lights in' he said.

My mother was preparing Sunday dinner. Peeling the potatoes, preparing the greens, mixing the batter and getting ready to put the brisket in the oven, she was listening to the Sunday morning service on the radiogram in the next room with the volume turned up when an announcement came that the Prime Minister was going to speak at 11.15. She called out the news to Dad.

'What do you think he's going to say?' she asked emotionally.

'I'll bet it's war' he replied bluntly. 'Jim next door thinks so as well.' I had heard Dad in conversation with the neighbours, in fact many of the men were out in their gardens. I had decided not to go to Sunday school that morning, but stayed in to listen to the momentous announcement.

At 11.15 the whole family were clustered round the radiogram when the old umbrella man started to speak in his tired voice.

'I am speaking to you from the cabinet room of number 10 Downing Street....'

The expression on my parent's faces became more solemn as the speech continued about withdrawing troops and an undertaking.

'....I have to tell you now that no such undertaking has been received and that consequently this country is at war with Germany....'

My mother was crying, my father was grim faced. The umbrella man had not been able to stop the war.

METHOD OF GAS-PROOFING A ROOM

APPLYING SEALING TAPE

Any type of room from cellar to attic may best be rendered gas proof by the use of an inexpensive, specially treated sealing tape which has been tested and found most suitable for this purpose. This tape can be kept indefinitely without perishing, and be used over and over again without losing its effectiveness. Your local ironmonger may be able to supply you with this material—known as Hermetyte; but should he not stock it, arrangements have been made with Winn and Coales, Ltd., of 40, Trinity Square, London, E.C.3, to supply any person privately who applies in person or by letter to their A.R.P. Dept. and mentions this A.R.P. monthly.

It is also possible to obtain gas-proofing materials in the form of putty and adhesive cord from the same source, but these materials are useful more for making a room permanently gas-tight.

The illustration above shows the sealing of a door. Two or three inches at the end of the roll of Hermetyte tape are pressed over the end of the crack to be sealed. The tape is unrolled in one hand while two fingers of the other hand—one on either side of the crack—are run down the tape for the whole length, pressing it firmly to the surface of the wood.

Hermetyte sticks to any material, and the above procedure is all that is necessary to ensure strong adherence and absolute safety. After use it may be peeled off and rolled up on the cardboard ring on which it is supplied.

CHAPTER TWO
SHINE YOUR TORCH DOWNWARDS

The second day of the war was a Monday, the first working day of the week.

'Don't forget your gas mask' Mum said to Dad, but he didn't have to be told: he already had it in the buff cardboard box along with his 'snap' as he called his packed sandwiches.

As school had not re-opened, I was off to call on a friend and noticed that most people were carrying gas masks. Mum made sure I had mine of course - any minute German planes could appear overhead and bomb and gas us, so I was taking no chances.

The familiar Ilkeston greeting 'Ey up mi duck' had given way to 'Got your gas mask' or in some cases 'Where's your gas mask?' When I went down to Bennerley Rec later that day with my friend we found that most of the other kids had them in their cardboard boxes with string attached and some had discovered that they made useful weapons by swinging them round at their enemies. One or two had specially designed covers in various types of material, especially the girls who had floral patterned ones. Later in the year I was given a metal container in a horrible mustard colour with the words GAS MASK inscribed on it. There was no law to make you carry a gas mask but at the beginning of the war we felt it was a duty.

No German planes appeared the first day and there were no air raid warnings although we heard on the news that some parts of the country including London had had an 'alert'. We felt sure that it wouldn't be long before 'Wailing Willie' or 'Moaning Minnie' as the sirens came to be called would soon be shattering our peaceful lives.

It was then that I decided to keep a war diary. Purchasing an exercise book from Gilbourne's the newsagents, I headed the first page SUNDAY 3RD SEPTEMBER in bold lettering with my Swan fountain pen, an 11th birthday present given to me by my parents the month before 'now that you've passed for Hallcroft School.' In my neatest writing I proceeded with my first entry: 'War declared. We heard Mr Chamberlain's speech saying we were at war with Germany and we all felt upset. Mum crying. Dad started digging a trench for us to use during air raids.'

That first week I diligently kept a record mainly gleaned from the papers. 'War Cabinet formed, Foreign Secretary Lord Halifax, First Lord of the Admiralty Winston Churchill.... Australia and New Zealand declare war on Germany.... Eire stays neutral.... Indiscriminate bombing of Poland by German Air Force.... Threat to Warsaw.... Six million leaflets entitled 'Note to the German people' dropped by RAF over North and West Germany.... Three million leaflets dropped on Ruhr.... RAF raid Wilhelmshaven and Kiel Canal, German battleship hit.... U-boats attacking our ships.... No air raids yet.... No sirens.... School not started up yet.... Played on Bennerley Rec.... All picture houses closed....'

The last entry came as a nasty shock. Everybody was outraged when the Government decided to close all cinemas, theatres, dance halls and places of entertainment.

'The one bit of pleasure we've got left' complained my mother who went to a weekly old-tyme dance. 'Surely there was no need to stop our entertainment.'

'And no pictures either' I grumbled. At the time I was going to the cinema two or three times a week. The four Ilkeston cinemas each had notices outside, CLOSED UNTIL FURTHER NOTICE. Cinema owners were up in arms. Eventually the Government decided to capitulate and by the end of September queues were once again outside for the re-opening so I was able to see George Formby in Trouble Brewing at the Kings while my mother took my sister Margaret to see Mickey Rooney in Adventures of Huckleberry Finn at the Ritz. Although cinemas, theatres and dance halls were back in business, some sports, notably greyhound racing and speedway, closed for the duration as they needed floodlighting.

In the early months of the war, the blackout was the real enemy. Although my mother and father had gone to a great deal of trouble putting thick curtains at the windows as the great majority of other families had, I remember a knock on the front door one evening when we were listening to the wireless. We looked at each other. Everyone we knew came to the back. On opening the door Dad was confronted with a warden.

'You're showing a light' the warden said.

On inspection, it turned out to be just a chink from the bathroom window where the curtaining had come adrift. I heard Dad being most apologetic - it didn't pay to be otherwise as the courts were busy dealing with blackout offenders - and we were let off with a caution. Those who were not so lucky were fined ten or fifteen shillings.

We had a relatively small semi-detached house but we felt sorry for those with large properties. Hardest hit were factories and business premises who had to spend large sums in blacking out. A. Booth & Sons, the Ilkeston hosiery firm, had spent £400 on blackout materials but they found themselves in court in October 1940 accused of permitting lights to show. They were found guilty but the magistrates were clearly sympathetic as they were only fined £1. The same month an Ilkeston householder protested after being fined the same amount. He had gone out leaving a light on during blackout hours. A passing policemen smashed one of his windows to gain entrance to put the light out.

We also heard about a party of Girl Guides camping at Marlpool. After their meal and camp fire sing-song they left without extinguishing the fire properly. Shortly afterwards it flared up and of course there was a warden on hand to bring the Guide leader to book. She was fined ten shillings.

Landlords of pubs had difficulty in enforcing the blackout. Customers leaving often disturbed the heavy curtains which had been put in place. If I walked along Cotmanhay Road in the evenings one of several pubs could be picked out from a distance.

But the worst was being out in the blackout. As soon as we stepped out of the house we were in a dark and alien world and could sometimes lose all sense of direction, even along streets and paths we thought we knew so well. People had the embarrassing experience of becoming lost in their own neighbourhood.

'Is this Milton Street, son?' I was asked.

'No it's Wesley Street. You want the next turning on this side past the chip shop.'

Council workers had been round painting kerbs, bollards, posts and belisha beacons either white or with white stripes but on the darkest nights this did not help much. Traffic lights and illuminated bollards were wearing shields showing only small crosses of light.

It was a relief when, about six weeks into the war, we were allowed to carry torches but they had to be dimmed with a double thickness of white tissue paper and not used at all during alerts. Still it was better than nothing.

'Remember to shine your torch downwards' ordered my father as I set off for the pictures on some winter evenings but it was always tempting to shine the torch at windows of houses or shops. Other kids were doing it and I had never seen any of them caught by a warden.

'Never mind what they're doing, don't you do it' was the order from Dad, always keen to keep to the letter of the law.

There soon became an acute shortage of batteries, both for torches and cycle lamps. There was a joke going round that raffles were being organised with torch batteries as prizes. They were prized items. I remember the triumphant look on Dad's face on several occasions on his return from work.

'Look what I've got' he said holding up a couple of torch batteries. 'Just got them from Deans. He's only letting his regulars have them though. Don't say anything.'

Life was made very difficult by the blackout and people grumbled all the time, especially during winter. We walked up and down Richmond Avenue by feeling our way along the stone or brick walls fronting the houses, but some streets were booby traps and there were many cases of pedestrians being injured by walking into walls, trees, telegraph poles, lamp posts, piles of sandbags and kerbs, or even just walking into other pedestrians. We got to know our neighbours better this way, but not really out of choice.

There were some tragic accidents. Under the heading COLLIDED WITH AIR RAID SHELTER we read in the Ilkeston Advertiser that on a dark night in December 1941 a 72 year old lady, Beatrice Reeve, was walking with her two daughters down Byron Street at 10 pm after visiting a relative. The four concrete shelters in the roadway had their corners painted white but there was no lighting. They were walking abreast without using torches, negotiated two of them but walked into the third, Mrs Reeve striking her head on the corner of the shelter. She died a fortnight later.

People in some parts of the country had been known to fall into rivers and canals - perhaps this happened in Ilkeston. Walking home from the pub at closing time had its problems for some people. Many tended to stay at home during the blackout, not just to listen to the wireless but to indulge in hobbies, games or pastimes.

It was an event when we acquired a dart board, one of the most popular games of the time. In our case it had to be carefully supervised as we were all very amateurish and my five year old brother was liable to pitch a dart in an unexpected direction so that the odds of being hit with a dart were much greater than being a target for one of Hitler's bombs. There was also the old favourites snakes and ladders and ludo, the card games of snap, progressing to whist, solo, brag and gin rummy which our parents invariably allowed us to win. I also had a craze on playing patience.

My mother always seemed to be knitting during the long evenings and she became a production line of jumpers, jerseys, cardigans, socks, hats and balaclavas. When wool became scarce and put on coupon, old woollen garments were unravelled and the wool re-used. Mum involved all of us in this, making the old wool into hanks which she then washed before knitting into other garments. Dad was making rugs, woollen ones with a hessian or sack base with a special 'pegger'.

Some people turned to music and piano playing which became extremely popular resulting in the singing of popular songs round the piano. Walking through the blackened streets in the evening I sometimes heard the loud refrain of Beer Barrel Polka and other favourites emanating from a darkened house. People were also taking up other instruments such as the violin, saxophone and clarinet. I never took up an instrument but was an avid reader and joined Ilkeston Public Library.

Occasionally I read the magazine Illustrated at a friend's house and in November 1939 I read an article 'Behind the Blackout in Acacia Avenue', purportedly portraying what people were up to during the long evenings. Of course reading was a popular pastime with a picture of Mr Lilley at number 13 sitting by the fireside in his slippers somewhat ambitiously reading volume one of Gibbon's 'Decline and Fall of the Roman Empire' (he expected it would take him three years to read all three volumes). I thought this was over-egging the pudding; I was content with Gibbons' Simplified Stamp Catalogue which I borrowed from my uncle, an ardent stamp collector who had introduced me to the hobby. I don't think I minded the blackout too much, there were plenty of things to do.

However, workers had to go out during the blackout. My father worked a shift system at British Celanese which meant that during the winter he was either going to or coming back from work during the blackout. The works bus left from Ash Street, nearly half a mile away, and he always left in good time with a margin to spare although I seem to remember a couple of occasions when he missed the bus after walking into obstacles, and several times he came home from work hobbling, limping, rubbing his shins or nursing a bruised shoulder ('this lamp post came up and hit me').

Some people suffered serious accidents and Ilkeston hospital was kept busy during the winters of 1939-40 and 1940-41, not with the casualties of war, but with the casualties of the blackout. In September 1939, the first month of war, 1,130 people lost their lives on the roads of Britain, more than double the figure for the same month in 1938.

'Do you realise there's more folks being killed on the roads than are being killed by Jerry, and that includes land, sea and air,' my uncle told me one day. He never owned a car, nor did my parents, in fact I knew of very few car owners in Cotmanhay during the war. Uncle Billy was a great one for statistics, gleaned from his Daily Sketch, John Bull, The Leader and Tit Bits and was always keen to impart the information. 'It's disgusting. The only war today is on the roads, nobody's bothering to fight like we did in the Great War, they're just killing each other on the roads instead.'

The Government were appealing to drivers to take greater care. Posters and newspaper advertisements were asking: How Many Will Die In The Blackout Tonight, while others urged: Look Out In The Blackout, with the warning: Remember - you can see the car when the driver can't see you. One poster showed a speedometer fixed at 20 mph with the slogan LESS LIGHT, LESS SPEED. Cars were allowed one screened headlamp but some people didn't seem to use lights at all.

'This car was right on top of me before I saw it. I had to jump for my life' I heard a neighbour telling Dad.

The silent running trolley buses in Ilkeston were also a bit of a menace; they were often on top of you before you realised when crossing the road.

Vera Brittain describes a journey she made in 1939 from Salisbury to Lyndhurst, about twenty miles, driving without lights through gathering darkness.

'We cannot see the signposts except by getting out of the car and striking a

20

match; we are guided away from the ditch only by the white line which divides the road, and springs into startling clearness whenever the car passes through the deep shadow of the woods. By the time we reach home I feel cramped and dizzy, but we arrive, miraculously, without mishap.'

Miraculous indeed. She was also lucky to find any signposts as they began taking them down in 1940. Driving on the roads at night was an ordeal. Petrol rationing was brought in on 23 September 1939 and was sufficient for car owners to do about a hundred and fifty miles a month. The petrol companies pooled their resources and consequently there was only one brand of petrol which was called Pool. Cars up to 7 horse power were allowed four gallons a month, 8 and 9 hp cars five gallons, rising to ten gallons for cars of 20 hp and over. Petrol then cost one shilling and sixpence a gallon and this gradually rose in price to two shillings and three halfpence by 1942. However if you needed petrol desperately you could always try the black market where it was available at about six shillings a gallon. Commercial petrol was dyed red to prevent it being used for private motoring but the spivs soon discovered how to remove the colour: pour it through your gas mask filter.

Another solution was to use alternative fuel as I discovered one day in December 1939 when I saw a car being driven with a large bag on the top. It was a weird sight and I wondered what it was in aid of.

'Oh it's Tommy Barton' I was told 'he's converted his car to gas. He's going to change some of his buses over to it.'

Mr Barton was the proprietor of Barton Transport which ran numerous bus services in the Nottingham, Ilkeston and Long Eaton districts and before long we began seeing his single deckers with gas bags on top and double deckers with bags on trailers behind. He had pioneered the idea in the first world war. His buses could run about forty miles with one filling of gas but carried petrol in case of breakdown.

There was great excitement one day in March 1941 when I heard from school friends that one of the Barton gas buses had crashed in Nottingham Road. Those living in the area described how they had seen the bus tipped over on its side near Thurman Street. Apparently it had been in collision with a couple of cars and probably the gas bag had made it unstable causing it to tip over, one of the drawbacks of this experiment. Five people were taken to hospital.

All kinds of new regulations were being brought in. Car bumpers and running boards had to be painted white, one headlamp had to be masked with a slit or several slits across it (the other headlamp had to have its bulb removed) and rear lights had to be dimmed. The idea seemed to be that the car should be seen rather than the driver being able to see where he was going. It was also suggested to motorists that they would see better if they opened up their windscreens, a very cold option in winter and not much better during the rest of the year.

As road deaths mounted the Government experimented with modified forms of street lighting and brought in a 20 mph speed limit during blackout hours from February 1940 but deaths continued to rise. In 1941 they were over 9,000 according to my uncle. Summer time was introduced in February 1940 and this was increased to Double Summer Time in 1941.

The Government were doing everything to discourage private motoring so it was a surprise to see an advertisement in the local paper from Elliott & Robinson of Stanley Common which incurred my father's wrath after he almost came into contact with a car speeding along Cotmanhay Road in the blackout.

'Look at this,' he said "'Be an asset to your country by learning to drive a car. No licence, no insurance, no car needed if you see us. We still have a few good used cars for sale at attractive prices." If you ask me there's enough lunatics on the road without encouraging learner drivers. And what do they mean, no licence and no insurance needed?' We discovered that driving tests had been suspended and anybody could apply for a wartime National Service Licence and learners could now drive unaccompanied and without L plates - probably a cause of the rising death rate on the roads.

In the early months of the war regulations were enforced rigorously. Motorists were fined for not having side lights screened and pedal cyclists for not having the front light screened. Typical fines were £2 for driving a car showing a white light from a fog lamp, ten shillings for not having side lights screened and five shillings for pedal cycling without the front light screened.

A woman before an Ilkeston court was accused of 'using motor fuel otherwise than with all reasonable economy.' A constable had found the engine of her car running for ten minutes while the car was stationery. In defence she said she had been advised to run the engine to make the batteries work.

A case which attracted widespread interest in the town was in June 1940 when Alderman Amos Henshaw, a magistrate and a member of Ilkeston Town Council, was summoned 'for acquiring a supply of motor spirit otherwise than against the surrender of valid coupons at Ilkeston on May 17th.' Conducting his own defence, Alderman Henshaw entered a plea of guilty to a technical offence and said his car ran out of petrol in Chapel Street near to a private petrol pump belonging to Mr F. Norman who was a friend. As Mr Norman was out he helped himself to the petrol and later told Mr Norman what he had done and would repay him with coupons dated for June and July. He admitted he had no coupons left for May. He was fine £1 and ordered to pay £2/2/- costs.

There was a scheme whereby motorists could volunteer to use their cars to help the war effort such as giving lifts to service men and women or taking evacuees to new homes. Thousands of vehicles were also mobilised for ambulance duties with the ARP and in London a third of the taxi fleet was taken over, many as staff cars for the armed forces.

There were still a few people motoring for pleasure which caused anger and indignation, especially when they saw pictures in the papers of a packed car park at the Derby race meeting and neighbours jaunting off at the weekend.

'They should be stopped' I overhead one woman say. 'My son's in the merchant navy risking his life to bring petrol so that these people can enjoy themselves. It's not right.'

In 1942 partly due to public pressure the basic ration was withdrawn altogether and petrol only allowed to those whose journeys were essential such as doctors and farmers but shopping in rural areas was allowed as were hospital visits and taking children to school. I read that some doctors were cycling on their rounds, but I don't remember our doctors - Sudbury and Myers at Galtee House - resorting to this method; I think it would have resulted in a loss of prestige. Of course many people were now using cycles and I often borrowed Dad's bike, not always with his permission.

There was a crackdown on any infringement of the strict new motoring laws and any driver could be stopped and asked to prove his journey was essential and even that he was travelling by the shortest route. There were heavy fines and some jail sentences: Ivor Novello the composer was jailed for four weeks for illegally using his car between his home and the London theatre where 'The Dancing Years' was being staged.

Other regulations which may sound trivial today included a ban on the striking of matches in the street which was liable to prosecution. As a smoker my father would wait until he came indoors before lighting up although he once told me that he had been stopped by a warden who told him 'put that cigarette out.' Dad, being easy-going and never courting trouble, complied, but I am sure some men may not have been so docile.

The blackout was a godsend to cartoonists and comedians adding much material to their repertoires, such as a policeman shining his torch into a doorway to discover a courting couple, the policeman saying 'What's all this?', the man replying 'Just giving the wife a cuddle, officer'. 'Are you sure it's your wife?' 'Not until you shone your torch, officer.' There was also a Blackout Book full of jokes, cartoons and puzzles. One newspaper ran a column 'Heard in the blackout' and I once saw a card game called Blackout 'the game to cheer you up, everybody's playing it.'

The real blackout was no game, it was a deadly serious business, very inconvenient and potentially dangerous. Maybe to us as children it did not seem too bad but to the rest of the population, especially the elderly, it was a nightmare.

23

Shopping
Sabotage

Mrs. Robinson is a sensible little body and as patriotic as they make 'em. But **yesterday she threw a spanner into the mechanism of our armaments production.**

It was sabotage—unconsciously done. Shopping in her home town the other day she bought some little thing she fancied but didn't really require. Now skilled men, machinery and factory organisation were used to make that thing, when they ought to have been making arms for victory.

In city, suburb and countryside people are still committing these unconscious acts of sabotage. Buying things they could really do without. Using up the men, materials and machines that the country needs so badly—and mark you—also helping to push up prices.

Make up your mind to censor your spending strictly—buying only those things that you urgently need. You will save money that should be lent to the Government to spend where it is needed—and (don't forget) your savings will earn good interest and will build up a useful fund for your future.

You can save by buying Savings Certificates, 3% Defence Bonds, 2½% National War Bonds, or by depositing in the Post Office or Trustee Savings Banks. Whichever way you choose make your savings as big as possible—save all you can.

Issued by the National Savings Committee, London.

CHAPTER THREE
HERE COMES THE NAVY

During the first few weeks of the war we were all tensed up waiting for something to happen. As soon as the sirens went we thought 'this is it' and took cover. But the Luftwaffe never appeared, we heard no planes, gunfire or bombs. Were they just having us on with all these false alarms? We were supposed to be in a war which had begun with all sorts of feverish activity, children had been evacuated, blackout curtains put in place, air raid shelters had been built, gas masks were carried everywhere, all kinds of new regulations had come in, but where was the war?

Dad had bought me a war map of Europe which I had hung on the kitchen wall. Countries were marked in different colours - Britain was red (of course), France was green, Germany purple and so on. I had been looking at Poland which was coloured orange. I read in the paper and wrote in my diary at the end of September that it had been captured by the Germans and the Russians so they had divided it and had half each. But Poland seemed a long way off. There were no armies fighting nearer home, nothing seemed to be happening in France except for what the wireless had called 'skirmishes'. As I looked at the map I was very impressed with the thick black line running along the eastern border of France and marked 'Maginot Line'.

'It's impregnable' Dad told me. 'Jerry won't get past that. It's got hundreds of miles of fortifications.'

Facing it and just over the German border was a series of dots marked 'Siegfried Line' which didn't look half as powerful. Besides, we would be sending troops to France (called the British Expeditionary Force, I was told) and so would the Empire countries, Canada, Australia, New Zealand, South

Africa and India. I particularly liked the idea of the Indians in their turbans and 'crack' Gurkha Regiment. They looked a fearsome lot. I saw a picture of them arriving in France later in the year with their columns of mules and pack horses and I felt sure they would get the better of Hitler's troops when the war started properly. No wonder we were singing

We're gonna hang out the washing on the Siegfried Line

Have you any dirty washing Mother dear

We're gonna hang out the washing on the Siegfried Line

'Cos the washing day is here

Listening to the wireless, we heard that our bombers had been dropping leaflets over Germany, condemning Nazi leaders, the idea being that the German people on hearing this would rise up, overthrow the Nazis and the war would end. Some chance.

'It's not bloody leaflets they should be dropping, it's bombs' was a remark I heard more than once in Ilkeston.

Let's give it to 'em proper' seemed to be a general sentiment.

But this is not what the Government were saying, according to Dad. When it was suggested the RAF should bomb the Ruhr, the industrial heart of Germany, Sir Kingsley Wood, the Air Minister, said that this was out of the question as the Ruhr's factories were private property! Dad said that sort of talk made him sick. Chamberlain was reluctant to sanction bombing fearing reprisals in which case Britain would come off worst as Germany had much the stronger air force, something like 4,500 first line aircraft against 2,000 British. These were the figures I saw in the papers which I copied in my diary.

Yet 'It'll all be over by Christmas' was an expression that was heard often during the first few weeks of war. Others thought differently although few anticipated a six year war. A Mass Observation survey showed that one in five thought the war would last less than six months, a similar number thought three years or more and two in five were 'don't knows.'

Feverish building activity on air raid shelters was bearing some fruit. Those at Granby Park, Sudbury Park and Rutland Rec were completed during the first month of the war and work was going ahead on those at Hilly Holies and Gordon Street. By the end of November 1939 shelters had been provided for 2,800 people - still less than ten per cent of the population. Work on school shelters had been given priority and at the beginning of the term in January 1940 all the planned 61 shelters had been constructed in the town and schools were back full time. There was some debate as to whether school shelters should be made available to members of the public but this was turned down by the Council in June 1940.

The residents of Shipley however had got together and constructed their own shelters. I had noticed a group of men with spades and shovels digging in a field at Hassock Lane and within a few weeks with plenty of graft and donations of cash and materials they had two shelters. Their 'number one'

26

accommodated seventy people with comfortable seating on each side and lit by electricity, 'number two' was smaller with candle power but had the luxury of carpets.

Many people were constructing their own shelters in back gardens. Mark Hallam, a builder of Little Hallam Lane, had been busy since the afternoon of the first day of war creating a shelter in his back garden, helped by his eight year old son Jeff. As he was digging, Tom Hardy who was passing called out: 'You won't need that Mark, the war won't last long enough.' How wrong that prophecy was to be as Tom would have to acknowledge when he became a special constable and a fire watcher as well as doing his normal job at Stanton Ironworks, occasional chimney sweeping and keeping pigs and poultry.

The Langton household however were not doing so well with their shelter. The winter rains had filled the trench with water and the project was abandoned in favour of the public shelter on Vernon Street, a quarter of a mile away, which had been built just before air raid warnings started. Some people were tempted to have professionally built shelters in their gardens after seeing advertisements from two Cotmanhay builders, Stapletons of Cotmanhay Road and Henshaws of Church Street, who were offering to build them 'from £10' but this was dismissed out of hand by Dad ('I'm not made o' money').

Others were lucky enough to be given Anderson shelters which seemed to be reserved for the southern end of the town, deemed to be in the most danger from bombing due to the proximity of Stanton. People were getting anxious about the lack of shelters and one of our more outspoken neighbours was helping to organise a petition for more shelters in the summer of 1940.

'When the bombing starts we shan't be safe in our own homes, we need proper shelters' he told us. People were only too pleased to sign the petition and he told us afterwards that well over two thousand people had signed and it was being presented to the Mayor at the Town Hall. People were also angry that some public shelters had been put in the wrong place, for instance those at Sudbury's Park and the Rutland Rec.

'They should be built where they are needed' was the message.

When air raids began in the summer of 1940 many families including ours went straight to the public shelters but the authorities appeared to discourage this by saying that the shelters were meant for people caught in the street during an alert. In June 1940 before the raids began members of the Town Council were saying that the safest place was indoors in the lower part of the house.

'If you get into a corner of your house near a wall and well away from windows so that no blast or broken glass can get you, you will be as safe as in an air raid shelter' the chairman of the ARP committee said, going on to stress the danger of hundreds of people rushing to air raid shelters in the blackout which could result in casualties.

Although not much had been happening on land or in the air, quite a lot was happening at sea. On the first day of war the liner Athenia with a thousand passengers outward bound from Britain was torpedoed by a U-boat and over a hundred people lost their lives.

'Just like the cowardly Germans' we were saying. 'They have to sink defenceless ships.'

However we all knew that we had the best navy in the world. The Royal Navy was the symbol of British strength and our naval blockade of the Germans would force them into starvation. That was what we were saying in the first few months of war. We all cheered when the cinema newsreels showed our warships pounding the enemy and escorting convoys, and I studied the details which appeared in newspapers and magazines of the strength of our forces. We had twelve battleships, three battle cruisers, seven aircraft carriers, 15 heavy cruisers, 45 light cruisers, 184 destroyers, 58 submarines and 27 motor torpedo boats. Our battleships were an awesome sight: even the names would bring terror to the enemy: Barham, Warspite, Valiant, Revenge, Repulse, Nelson, Rodney, Ramillies, Resolution, Royal Oak and the mighty Hood, the largest warship in the world. Then there were our aircraft carriers: Ark Royal, and the newly-built Illustrious and Victorious, each carrying 36 planes to dive-bomb the enemy, as well as the older carriers Courageous and Glorious.

I studied the fire power of our naval forces and it was obvious we were so much more powerful than the Germans. They had a couple of battleships, the Scharnhorst and the Gneisnau, which seemed to spend most of their time sheltering in harbours, and they only had seven cruisers and 21 destroyers. Admittedly they had more submarines, about 160, which they called U boats but I was sure our warships could deal with them. No wonder when we played our games of naval warfare in the streets, nobody wanted to be the Germans.

But a shock was in store. Two weeks into the war Courageous was torpedoed and I felt very sad when I saw a picture in the paper of her keeling over. Five hundred sailors lost their lives. Another shock came a few weeks later in October when a U-boat managed to penetrate the Royal Naval base of Scapa Flow in the north of Scotland and sank the great battleship Royal Oak. It went down in 13 minutes after U47 struck it with two torpedoes. We read that men were thrown into the water thick with furnace oil which made swimming to the shore almost impossible although it was only a mile and a half away. My diary entries seemed to be all bad news.

'They caught us with our pants down' said Uncle Billy. 'They should remember what happened in the Great War after we'd captured the German fleet. We put them into Scapa and then let the Germans scuttle the lot. They out-smarted us then, now they've done it again.'

My diary was also recording that the U-boats were sinking our merchant ships and many lives were being lost in spite of our great navy. It all seemed bad news until one day in December when we heard about the German pocket-battleship Graf Spee. There had been a battle in the South Atlantic, three of our cruisers against the Graf Spee which had been badly damaged and driven into Montevideo harbour where it was being repaired. The government of Uruguay announced that it would allow the Graf Spee a stay of just 48 hours, then it would have to leave to face the fire power of the British forces waiting outside the harbour.

Here was some real excitement, a great naval battle was in the offing as I studied the newspaper reports. The three allied cruisers were HMS Exeter, HMS Ajax and the New Zealander HMNZS Achilles. The Exeter had already been seriously damaged and Ajax had lost half its guns but other British warships including the cruiser HMS Cumberland were already racing to the mouth of the River Plate to do battle.

The Royal Navy had been trying to catch the Graf Spee for months. It was the pride of the German navy and had spent the first three months of the war in the South Atlantic attacking British ships and had actually sunk nine including the liner Doric Star. It was a formidable enemy with six 11 inch guns and eight six inch and had thick protective plating. At last it had been cornered but our cruisers were more lightly armed: the Exeter had six 8 inch guns and four 4 inch, and our other two cruisers had eight 6 inch and eight 4 inch. These were the details we were studying as we read every paper and listened to every news bulletin.

Sixty two survivors of the nine British ships the Graf Spee had sunk were released in Montevideo. On 15 December the Uruguayan government announced it would allow another 24 hours for the ship to remain in harbour, then it would either have to leave or be interned for the rest of the war. As excitement built up, we heard that enormous crowds were taking up positions along the estuary of the River Plate to view the ensuing battle and there were reports that plane loads of Americans were flying in to watch.

We were tuned into the bulletins on the wireless all the time waiting for news of the great naval battle about to take place. But we were to be disappointed. The Graf Spee finally put to sea at 6.30 on the evening of 17 December with a skeleton crew. Seventy minutes later she was blown up and sank about five miles outside the harbour. So she went down without a fight. The following night her commander, Captain Langsdorff, shot himself in Buenos Aires and the crew of a thousand were interned in Argentina for the rest of the war.

My thoughts were now on Christmas, in fact they had been for a week or two, ever since I looked in Harry Whitehead's window and saw his display of Meccano, Hornby trains and Dinky toys. I had been building up a stock of Meccano over the years by Christmas and birthday presents and could now construct all kinds of elaborate creations such as cranes, gantries, big wheels and other fairground rides, even Blackpool Tower with a working lift, and there was usually one of these proudly displayed on the sideboard or even in the front room window.

Last year I had set number 5, this year it had to be set number 6 which had a wider and larger range of pieces. It was not an easy decision as there was also a tempting Hornby loco in green livery which would enhance my train set, but I had been warned there was a strict financial limit which meant I could not have both. It would have to be the Meccano but I might be able to wheedle some track and a set of points as well. There was also a book of warplanes I had my eye on, then there was one on warships, another on tanks.... oh, what decisions had to be made.

I had to get presents for my parents of course. Dad was easy: it had to be a packet of twenty Craven A cork tipped, the only cigarettes he was really happy smoking, although later in the war when cigarettes became scarce and disappeared under the counter he had to resort to Players, Weights or Gold Flake and I even knew him to smoke Woodbines and Park Drive, but he drew the line at Pashas. Mum had to get the cigarettes of course as children weren't allowed to buy them, but Mum's present was a little more difficult to choose. Looking in the window of Novelty Shop (I was diffident about entering) I saw various ladies' items on display most of which were either outside my price range or required knowledge of sizing. There were handbags, stockings, underwear, sweaters and furs but I did note a few cheaper items including gloves, umbrellas, even coat hangers. However I decided against them and moved on to Timothy Whites where I saw canteens of cutlery at 18/11d, electric fires at 5/- and cakestands at 3/11d, all of which were outside my price range. Eventually I settled for a bottle of scent and a box of Phul-Nana face powder from Woolworths.

Christmas Day was celebrated much the same as in previous years. We tucked in to pork and stuffing (we never had poultry at Christmas) and plum pudding and afterwards sat and listened to the King's speech. I started building a large gantry with my Meccano set while my young brother Trevor played with a new Hornby train set while sister Margaret was nursing a new doll. I noticed some of the boys in the neighbourhood were playing with toy soldiers and one had a model Maginot Line. Dad had treated himself to some gramophone records and these were played continually throughout Christmas so that by the end of festivities we knew every word of Run Rabbit Run, Beer Barrel Polka, Sing As We Go and the Hut Sut Song. My mother was placated by a recording of The Holy City and Sanctuary of the Heart.

Temporarily we forgot the blackout and Hitler. We heard that many evacuees had gone home, not that there were any in Ilkeston, but in the reception areas they had been returning in droves all through November and December. The reasons for their return was that there had been no bombing and also that the Government had started to demand a contribution from parents to support their evacuated children. By the first week in January 1940 900,000 of the one and a half million evacuated in September had returned home.

January 1940 was one of the coldest months on record. Everything froze. Roads were impassable. Our parents hated the appalling weather, but for us children there were compensations. We indulged in snowball fights, made sledges out of pieces of wood or old orange boxes (there were still a few around in 1940 although there were no oranges) or created slides in the street in spite of threats from parents.

At school we were warned off snowballing and making slides, but the ice-bound playground held traps for the unwary as I discovered one day, falling flat on my face, knocking out a front tooth, bruising my face and chin and left feeling badly shaken. One of the teachers looked at me, told me I would live and ordered me to carry on. However, they did make an appointment with the school dentist who removed the root of the tooth after his assistant told me I had a dirty face and chin. Apparently, she couldn't tell the difference between dirt and bruising. Mishaps at school in the 1940s were often treated with indifference.

Public transport almost ground to a halt during the ice-bound winter. We were back at school full time but the problem was getting there. Most mornings we awoke to find another layer of snow and the first task of the day was to dig ourselves out. It was about fifteen yards from the back door to the front gate and a path had to be cleared with spades and shovels.

On several occasions that winter my recollections are of snow over a foot high round the house and as we worked in clearing it the sound of scraping shovels jarred across a white world. There was a community spirit as men cleared the paths of elderly neighbours too frail to do the job. Frontages also had to be cleared for the benefit of the postman and milkman and when we were clear it was off to school and work, hoping that the trolley bus service was still in operation.

The buses ploughed their way gingerly, stopping to pick up passengers and occasionally for the driver to re-instate the poles with the crackling of electrical sparks. Town traffic was just about able to cope but some drivers refused to stop on hills as they could not get started again.

'Next stop Market Place' was the conductresses cry at Pelham Street.

'But I want Station Road.'

'Then you'll have to slide back down Bath Street.'

There was much grumbling but people were secretly thankful that at least buses were running in the town whereas the Ilkeston-Derby service had to be abandoned at one stage as the road was closed in several places.

Every bus was packed with passengers now that almost everybody relied on public transport. Priority was given to workers and shoppers were urged to travel only between 10 in the morning and 4 in the afternoon.

'Workers only' was the cry heard in the early mornings and late afternoons as the bus pulled up to the stop. Men and women in overalls and working clothes pressed forward leaving shoppers and schoolchildren behind. It was sometimes difficult to tell who were the workers and arguments frequently developed with a harassed conductor attempting to arbitrate. People travelling a long distance thought they should be given priority over those travelling a few stops and I witnessed many ill-tempered scenes. I also witnessed considerate passengers leaving the bus prematurely to let a waiting passenger get on ('I'm only going to Archer Street, I can walk this last bit').

Ilkeston had many working miners at the time and they were given absolute priority - still in their pit dirt before the introduction of pit head baths. In consideration of other passengers, they never took seats, standing in the aisle and keeping their distance from others.

The rule limiting the number of standing passengers was relaxed, in fact almost totally disregarded, and I saw well over a dozen standing on some buses, making it very difficult even for the conductor to collect fares. Life for the conductors became very difficult and as time went by and men were called up they gave way to women or 'clippies' as we called them.

During the evenings the interiors of the buses were lit only by dimmed bulbs which cast a bluish glow, an opportunity for the unscrupulous to pass dud coins. Through it all the majority of the conductors and clippies remained cheerful and helpful and we got to know them very well. There was often good-natured banter on the most crowded of vehicles, even from standing passengers with elbows and shopping baskets pushed in their ribs.

MARKET PLACE, ILKESTON.

Give them all *Craven 'A'* this Xmas

25 *for* 1/5½
40 *for* 2/4
50 *for* 2/11
100 *for* 5/10
150 *for* 8/9
200 *for* 11/8

MORE and more people are smoking Craven 'A' because these famous Cork - Tipped cigarettes are so fresh, cool—smooth to the throat. You can be certain you are choosing a gift which will be thoroughly appreciated if you send all your friends Craven 'A' this Christmas.

FLAT POCKET TIN.
50 *for* 2/11

MADE SPECIALLY TO PREVENT SORE THROATS

33

CHAPTER FOUR
WAIT FOR THE WHISTLE

Education disintegrated during the first few months of the war. Ilkeston schools, like those in many other towns, did not reopen on Monday 4 September. Some had been taken over partially by the Civil Defence services, others had insufficient or no air raid shelters to satisfy ARP regulations.

As children we saw no great hardship in this. Some kids were running wild, up to all kinds of mischief including vandalising newly-built shelters which were often kept locked. I spent part of my time in the first two months of the war on nearby Bennerley Recreation Ground with games of football where coats served as goalposts and cricket where sticks were improvised for stumps. Short breaks were taken watching old men playing bowls on the green.

My sister, brother and I often teamed up with the Elliott children next door who were of similar ages to the three of us. Ivan, the eldest, was the adventurous one who usually knew a little used path. We made sorties into Shipley and Cotmanhay woods, occasionally up to Shipley Hall, the former home of the Miller-Mundys but now a ruin, and then there were three canals to explore, the Erewash, the Nottingham and the Nutbrook, where we could play daring games such as walking across the locks although I always chickened out of this, heeding the threats of my mother.

My sister Margaret was usually content with staying around the house or garden having dolls' teaparties with Violet from next door, while my four year old brother Trevor found a playmate in young Arnold.

On rainy days we stayed in and read comics. By a well organised swop system we were able to keep up with our favourite characters. Many of the comics finished up dog-eared, torn or stained (or all three) much to the disgust of my parents ('Where did you get that filthy thing from' or 'That's only fit for the dustbin') but I was seldom deterred.

I kept up with the doings of Basil and Bert, 'very' private detectives in the Jester, a penny comic printed on pink paper which my Uncle Billy took and which he kept in near-perfect condition. I was allowed to read it at weekends, the front page devoted to the strange pair of detectives, Basil dressed like a toff and sporting a monocle while his unlikely companion had unkempt hair. Every week they were on secret service duty in Nastyland, always getting the better of Ateful Adolph, General Snoring, Herr von Drippingtop and Herr Gobbles.

Other characters were also helping the war effort. Constable Cuddlecook was now wearing a tin hat and even Cinderella and Her Artful Sisters were getting mixed up with the military, Cinderella invariably dated by the most handsome officer. One Saturday in May 1940 I went round to Uncle Billy's to discover the Jester had not arrived. Uncle told me the sad news: it had ceased publication, a casualty of the war and shortage of newsprint. It never returned.

One comic which did continue throughout the war (until 1953 in fact) was Illustrated Chips or simply Chips as we called it. This had been going since 1890 with the famous characters, Weary Willie and Tired Tim, a couple of amiable tramps created by the artist Tom Browne. They had done service in two wars - the Boer War and the Great War of 1914-18 - and now they were having to face food shortages of the Hitler war but they got by, even though it did mean hanging around the cookhouse door or waiting for tins of bully beef to drop off an army lorry.

A twopenny comic, the Knockout, appeared in March 1939 and soon grabbed our attention, even when its price rose to threepence in 1941. This featured Deed-a-Day Danny, ever eager to help the war effort but never quite turning out as expected, and Stonehenge Kit, the Ancient Brit, although living in the stone age, she had to deal with tanks made of stone. In May 1940 the famous boys' paper, the Magnet, founded in 1908 and with nearly 1,700 issues behind it, joined forces with the Knockout and with it went Billy Bunter, 'the fattest schoolboy on earth.'

Film Fun, founded in 1920, is remembered for its Laurel and Hardy strip which first appeared on the front page in 1934 (and continued on the back page). Of course they joined the army like most of the other Film Fun characters: Joe E. Brown, Harold Lloyd, Lupino Lane, Claude Hulbert and others, while Old Mother Riley was helping on the home front.

The most popular comic of all however was the Beano. First issued in 1938 by the Scottish publisher D.C. Thomson, it had a colourful front cover given to the exploits of Big Eggo, an ostrich, which had also enlisted to help the allies, each week outwitting the enemy. This comic also included the Italian dictator Mussolini who was portrayed as an incompetent under the title 'Musso the Wop, He's a big-a-da-Flop,' a phrase which was constantly repeated in playgrounds all over the country.

In the same comic Lord Snooty and His Pals were a strange assortment of friends. Headed by the top-hatted Lord Marmaduke - 'Snooty to you' as the comic would have it - they comprised Hairpin Huggins, Scrapper Smith,

Happy Hutton, Skinny Lizzie, Rosie, Snitchy and Snatchy and usually bringing up the rear was Gertie the goat. A similar cartoon in the sister comic, the Dandy, was entitled Our Gang with another unlikely lot of characters. Every week they entertained us along with Korky the Kat, Pansy Potter ('the strong man's daughter'), Desperate Dan and many others. With all these characters on our side, how could we fail to win the war?

However, my parents were not impressed. 'You should be studying, not idling about and reading this rubbish. Read some books or study your atlas.' This criticism was followed by a decision on their part of what my next Christmas present would be: the Complete Self-Educator.

As an avid reader I had joined the public library which had been hit by a loss of staff: the Borough Librarian reported that 60% had been transferred to ARP duties and the lending department had reduced its daily hours to 10 am to 1 pm and 4 to 7 pm. I used the children's department on the first floor, a holy of holies where you could only speak in whispers and a large SILENCE notice was affixed to the wall. My preference was for adventure stories and I went through whole series of books with daring deeds of aviators such as Biggles and the American counterpart, Ted Scott.

I noticed that school teachers were now doing ARP work. Some had become wardens, others were doing the gas mask census or acting as billeting officers. Others were involved in administration: there was plenty of paperwork. No computers or word processors to help in those days!

Three of the biggest schools in the town - Bennerley, Chaucer and Cavendish - were partially requisitioned for first aid posts. Add to this the loss of Hallam Fields School which was closed due to its proximity to Stanton, now producing bombs and military equipment. I had attended Hallam Fields School five years previously. It was situated in an ancient building in the shadow of the ironworks where the staff fought a losing battle with dirt and grime. The feeling was that it should have been condemned years previously. Shipley School, too, was closed due to mining subsidence, the underground tunnels now worked out but the building itself creaking with the result. What this meant was that a large proportion of school accommodation in Ilkeston had gone.

The spacious Bennerley Schools were now limited to four classrooms and worked on a shift basis, boys in the mornings, girls in the afternoons (the sexes were divided at Bennerley anyway); two classes were jammed into one room. Cavendish seniors were accommodated at the condemned St Mary's Schools which we heard was rat-infested; it was close to the old churchyard and had been empty for years. Gladstone seniors took junior and infants pupils from Chaucer which involved a long walk for many of them, while Hallam Fields pupils were the worst off of all: they were relocated to the Catholic School, a considerable distance for infant and junior children. Parents with strong religious feelings were none too happy with the arrangement either.

Even before these arrangements came into force, the Education Committee of Ilkeston Borough Council - for these were the days prior to the 1944

Education Act when Ilkeston controlled its own education - decided to organise classes in private houses. Offers from fifty people had been received and twenty five of these had been taken up. It was a makeshift system with children of varying ages being given lessons, about a dozen at a time, but probably better than no lessons at all. Gladstone pupils in particular were using this system as the school had not reassembled by late October. Other local authorities were resorting to temporary arrangements, for instance in Nottingham the three hundred boys from Radford Boulevard Schools were being taught in five rooms at Wollaton Hall which was still open to the public.

I had been rather looking forward to starting at Hallcroft but here I was, school cap and blazer at the ready, spending my days on Bennerley Rec or the canal bank or reading library books and comics. Although we were at war there were no exciting happenings, no guns or Spitfires shooting down enemy planes, only a few Tiger Moth training planes from Hucknall buzzing around and the only times the sirens went were for practice or false alarms.

Hallcroft had a problem: there were no air raid shelters. The plan had been to build shelters in the playgrounds - there were separate boys' and girls' schools divided by a high brick wall - but it was discovered there was a drainage problem which ruled it out so land had to be purchased adjoining the schools. This took time of course and it was October before building commenced.

The following month word came to start school part-time. I arrived at the almost deserted school clutching my gas mask and followed a chalked notice to find myself in a classroom with twenty or thirty other boys and a teacher. We were given homework and told to bring it back completed a few days later at a specified time. It seemed strange attending school for no more than half an hour, briefly meeting my new teacher, Mr Webster, and my new classmates. As the shelters began to be completed we went for half a day, some in the mornings, some afternoons. It was not until the following January when all the underground shelters had been built that we went full-time.

Like all other schools Hallcroft was surrounded by sandbags and netting covered the windows to prevent splintering from bomb blast. The result was that classrooms were very dark and lights seemed to be switched on permanently and I don't think the windows were ever cleaned.

One of the teachers I knew quite well. He was Frank Noon, music and geography teacher who lived in the next road to us and a member of the Wesley Methodist Church which I attended. He was an organist there, a large genial man, fair but firm in his dealings, who commanded respect from the boys at Hallcroft who knew he would stand no nonsense. I also remember he was a warden who patrolled the streets of Cotmanhay during 'alerts.' On one occasion during a long 'alert' period we had come outside to see if there was any activity and were talking to the neighbours in the small hours of the morning.

'Not heard Jerry tonight.'

'Probably gone to Liverpool by another route.' A favourite target for German planes was Merseyside and they often came over our area.

'We'll hear 'em coming back then.'

We saw the looming figure of Frank Noon. 'You people should be indoors, it can be dangerous out here during an alert.'

Reluctantly we all went back inside, the grown-ups chuntering 'who does he think he is,' although they knew he was right.

There was a serious shortage of school teachers during the war. Some had joined the Forces on the outbreak, others had been called up. There were no new recruits from training colleges so the gap was largely filled by married women who had left the profession, but during my two years at Hallcroft I don't recall any women teachers, although when I went to the Ilkeston County Secondary School in 1941 there were several.

Headmaster at Hallcroft was Thomas Ball, an amiable man with strong local connections. His father kept a pork butcher's shop in the town and his wife was a member of the town council. He had been appointed head in 1936 after teaching general subjects at the school, mainly to junior classes. He was well liked and my impression was that he was easy going for a head.

I started off in Form 1A. The form master was Alan Robert Webster who took us for maths, science, scripture and physical training. I soon settled into the routine of the school but it came as a shock when Mr Webster suddenly died in September 1940. He was teaching on a Wednesday and complained of not feeling well so took the afternoon off. Imagine the shock the following day when the school was told he had died overnight. Only 29, he was a native of Ilkeston and had taught at Hallcroft five or six years. He was married with a year-old baby. The funeral on 30 September was attended by the ARP - he was an air raid warden in the town - civil defence and some of our teachers. Each class sent a wreath.

The teaching staff at Hallcroft during the two years I was there were professional and competent and these included Messrs Nash (French), McIntyre (art), 'Sol' Smith (science), Jones (maths), Wallbank (history), Mann (English) and Walford (handicrafts).

Austin Dennis Nash or ADN (changed to 'A Damned Nuisance' by the boys - one of the kindlier epithets) was our form master for a year and the teacher we most feared. He had a short fuse and woe betide the boy who crossed him: he was invariably punished with the strap. Mr Nash set high standards and expected others to do likewise and I particularly remember one morning when half the class including myself turned up late. We were lined up in front of the others and given a verbal lashing: we were lazy idle good-for-nothings, we were lily-livered and had a variety of shortcomings which he enumerated in some detail, and were warned in no uncertain terms never to be late again. The fact that there had been an air raid alert during the night lasting till about five o'clock in the morning when we had spent the time in air raid shelters was not a valid excuse for ADN. He was at school on time; so should everybody else be. The official position on this point was given by the Director of Education that it was in order for pupils to go to school late following an air raid. Parents who had been keeping their children off school for the whole of the morning were advised: 'Send your children to school however late they may be.' So put that in your pipe and smoke it Mr Nash, we thought, although none of us were brave enough to tell him.

After I left Hallcroft in the summer of 1941 Mr Nash was appointed head, although many thought this should have gone to the deputy head at the time, Glynne Jones.

Welcome diversions at school were regular air raid drills when we would rise in our seats on hearing the blast of the whistle and march out in orderly fashion, class by class through the playground to the shelters where we would stay for several minutes before being escorted back by the teachers. These sessions were very popular, especially when they came in the middle of some unpopular lesson.

When the real thing occurred it didn't quite go according to plan. On one memorable occasion in the middle of a lesson we suddenly heard several loud bangs.

'Bombs!' yelled one of my classmates leaping to his feet.

'Sit down you fool' roared the teacher.

Seconds later we hear the piercing whistle from the main hall (there had been no warning siren).

'All stand' said the red-faced teacher, with some boys quietly smirking at the volte-face. 'Next time you wait for the whistle.'

We filed into the playground to be greeted with the spectacle of a Heinkel bomber right overhead with shells from anti-aircraft guns exploding round it. We just stood there gawping. It was much better than the pictures: we were seeing the real action.

'Down him! Down him!' we yelled.

When the teacher at the head of the column realised he had lost most of his charges, he went mad.

'Get in these shelters' he roared. 'You'll all be KILLED.'

We heard later that the lone German raider had jettisoned its bombs and was making for home but shortly afterwards was shot down by one of our fighters. But to a group of boys at Hallcroft, it was one of the most exciting events of the war.

School dinners were a new innovation for us in January 1940. In Ilkeston, only Gladstone had such facilities, in fact they had been providing meals for necessitous children during the 1920s and 1930s. As Hallcroft almost adjoined Gladstone, we began taking a cooked mid-day meal at Gladstone. At first there were only a few of us from Hallcroft and it was rather a makeshift affair but as the weeks went by numbers increased, extra kitchen staff brought in and eventually meals were served at Hallcroft itself although the cooking was still done at Gladstone.

Catering for children was never easy and in wartime it was doubly difficult with little variety. Soggy potatoes, strange tasting rissoles, gravy that you could almost slice and suet puddings appeared with monotonous regularity.

'What's this?' asked a new boy.

'Tapioca.'

'Looks like snot.'

If such remarks were overheard by the canteen staff a rumpus ensued.

Other schools also began serving school meals and at one time Gladstone was supplying 1,500 hot meals a day. They were transported in suitable cartons to the various schools in a Morris 30 cwt van with special fixtures and fittings capable of carrying up to 700 meals a day. Later another kitchen was opened at Cavendish which could supply 500 meals a day.

School holidays of course were the highlight of the year but in the early part of the war some holidays were curtailed. I suppose the authorities thought we had missed so much schooling during the autumn of 1939 that there was some catching up to be done. Because of the national emergency, the August Bank Holiday of 1940 was cancelled (although some workers took time off). In Ilkeston the normal midsummer school holiday of a month was restricted to two full weeks: we broke up on the 2nd and returned on 20 August. Few families went away.

Government advice not to travel but to have 'stay at home' holidays resulted in local councils organising various events. There was an 'Ilkeston Games Week' in July 1941 designed to promote fitness amongst young people between the ages of 14 and 20 and also to provide entertainment for the town's people in general. Sport was not one of my enthusiasms, in fact throughout my school life I prevailed on my parents to write notes to p.t. and games teachers giving reasons, nearly all spurious, as to why I was unavailable for football, cricket, swimming, physical jerks etc (colds, sore throat, flu, bad leg etc). I did actually go along to the Rutland Rec during Games Week armed with a library book and a bag of sweets and I read in the paper afterwards that at one time three hundred young people were playing some kind of organised game.

Another event at which I kept a low profile was Hallcroft School sports day when we all trooped to the Rutland Rec to admire the athletic types running, jumping and three-legging it to gain points for various 'houses' which for some reason not apparent to us were named after the ancient Greeks. Thus, I was an Athenian, expected to cheer on and applaud my fellow Athenians, but Monday 28 July 1941 was a bad day for them - the result, 1 Corinthians, 2 Spartans, 3 Olympians, 4 Athenians, seemed to suggest that the Athenians were lacking in prowess, unlike their namesakes two thousand five hundred years previously.

Another diversion from lessons was Empire Day which was celebrated every year on 24 May. During the war this took on added importance as all the countries in the British Empire were also at war with Germany. In 1941 every school in Ilkeston received a visit from the Mayor and a 'special visitor'; in Hallcroft's case it was Councillor G.W. Wooliscroft who told us how important 'our Empire' was and how the Canadians, Australians, New Zealanders, South Africans and Indians were coming to the aid of the mother country. All good patriotic stuff which went down well as we missed a couple of lessons.

Hallcroft also had a thriving drama group which seemed to be comprised mainly of ex-pupils and was led by one of the masters, V. Keeling Mann. Regular public performances were put on and during the first week of August 1941 a large audience watched 'As You Like It' on Victoria Park, an attempt to bring culture to the masses. We were so short of live entertainment that I think any such event would have done well.

One school which did not come within the jurisdiction of the Education Committee was Michael House in Heanor Road. This was a private school opened before the war providing an education based on the principles of Dr Rudolph Steiner, born in Austria in 1861, who had delivered 6,000 lectures on the Science of Spirit or Anthroposophy from the turn of the century until his death in 1925. His concept of education (sometimes called Waldorf Education) was to prepare the child for an eventual role as a resourceful, creative and responsible member of a modern society by encouraging their natural development rather than the competitive element of other schools which put the accent on testing and examinations.

Schools had been opened on the continent, the most important at Dornach in Switzerland, and the school at Ilkeston was one of the first to be opened in this country. In 1939 and 1940 I noticed it being rebuilt and the style of architecture drew a fair amount of comment as it did not look like a school at all; it had graceful lines which gave it a dignified appearance, more like a concert hall.

The pupils however became the butt of insults and jokes from groups of other schoolchildren in the town, which appeared to stem from the fact that they had German and Austrian teachers and they were taught German as a language. Coming out of school they were met with Nazi salutes and Heil Hitler's. Like racism today it was very hard to check. Of course there were no justification for the taunts, in fact some of the teachers had fled from the Nazis. To add insult to injury, I believe some teachers were detained as aliens in a very heavy-handed move by the Government which caused considerable outrage.

The new school building was opened in May 1940 by Miss E.G. Wilson followed by a two day festival of lectures and music. A dozen years later I married one of the pupils.

Their first children— THREE BOYS

Most mothers who have taken in evacuated children know how to cater for them, but when a childless couple had three hungry boys on their hands it wasn't so easy.

'My husband and I have always wanted children, though we have none of our own,' says Mrs. Nancy Cragg, wife of a Newark coal merchant. 'So when the evacuation plans were made we offered our home to three little Sheffield boys—Malcolm, aged 9, Donald, 9, and Brian, 6. It was a bit of a shock at first having suddenly to cope with a full-size family and I didn't see how the money was going to stretch out. Then I read the Bournville advertisements. My word, how those boys tuck into their Bournville Cocoa! And it's doing them a power of good. It's not only a drink, it's a food and it costs practically nothing.'

CADBURY'S

42

CHAPTER FIVE
SPREAD THE BUTTER THINLY

During the last months of 1939 the good people of Ilkeston, like others throughout Britain, were stocking up on sugar and tinned meats.

When I went into the pantry I noticed that the usual two packets of red label tea had now grown to five, there were several blue bags of sugar instead of the usual one and tins of ham, tongue and a John West's salmon had appeared on one shelf which had previously accommodated home made cakes and tarts.

'Ooh lovely' was my reaction on seeing the salmon. 'Are we having company?' I knew the only time we indulged in salmon was when aunts and uncles came.

'No we're not' retorted my mother, 'we're saving it for when things get short.'

The John West's salmon was clearly for hoarding rather than eating. Likewise mum was making sure that we would never be without our cuppa: dad in particular was a great tea drinker as most manual workers were.

Everybody was hoarding and the richer you were the more you could hoard. All kinds of stories were circulating such as a friend of a friend who knew someone who had five bedrooms and three of them were full of food, 'enough to stock a shop.'

In November the ration books arrived with coupons for basic foods and we were told to register with retailers for bacon, ham and butter which had now become short. By mid December 31,000 ration books had been issued in Ilkeston, practically the whole population, and people were registering with their favourite retailers. Our loyalties were divided between the Ilkeston Co-op and Jefferies, a good class grocer who specialised in bacon and cooked meats.

The Co-op was very strong in Ilkeston with many branches - a huge new store had just been opened adjoining the Market Place - and there was the attraction of 'divi' which was a dividend (about 10% at the time) paid to members on all purchases. There had been a 'scare' during the first few weeks of war that the Co-op would no longer be paying 'divi' which led to an announcement in the Ilkeston Advertiser of 20 October that the rumours were 'entirely baseless and false', much to the relief of many townspeople, some of whom seemed to be more concerned about this than the sinking of the Royal Oak at Scapa Flow. Now that 'divi' was assured Ilkeston responded by registering at the Co-op: 14,000 of them for bacon, 18,000 for butter and 19,000 for sugar. In other words, well over half the population bought their groceries from the Co-op. I wonder what it is today.

A large advertisement on the front page of the Ilkeston Advertiser headed REASONS FOR RATIONING explained that half our meat and most of our bacon, butter and sugar came from overseas and rationing prevented food wastage, increased our war effort, divided supplies equally and prevented uncertainty.

We knew rationing had been coming and most people welcomed the food controls including maximum prices; they much preferred a guaranteed amount of food at a fixed price rather than a free for all where the rich would build up their stockpiles and the rest would go hungry. Only the Daily Express seemed to be against rationing calling it 'that dreadful and terrible inequity which some ministers want to adopt'. But Dad took the Daily Herald, a Labour paper, although I am not sure whether he took it for its politics or for the racing tips of Templegate.

The weekly ration was fixed at four ounces of butter, twelve ounces of sugar (reduced to eight in May), four ounces of uncooked bacon or ham and three and a half ounces of cooked ham.

My mother had a very strict eye for any extravagance or wastage of food. 'A pound and a quarter of butter and that's got to last the five of us all week, so don't let me catch any of you wasting it' she warned as she scraped it on the bread and then proceeded to scrape most of it off again. There was no fear of us wasting butter I thought as I watched her retrieving every morsel from the wrapping paper. Of course there was Stork Margarine which my mother was now reluctantly buying: she had always regarded margarine as a second rate substitute.

Meat was getting short and in March 1940 rationing began with one shilling and tenpence worth for adults (later reduced to one shilling and a penny) and elevenpence for small children. The following month Lord Woolton became the Minister of Food who turned out to be one of the most popular members of the Government with his easy manner and chatty broadcasts and hints on making the most of rations. My mother often listened to an early morning programme, The Kitchen Front, which gave recipes in a light-hearted sort of way. I remember once listening to the programme which featured Elsie and Doris Waters, a couple of comedians who called themselves 'Gert and Daisy' chatting away with Lord Woolton himself and telling him how they made the most of their one and tenpence worth of meat.

There were also newspaper adverts and Food Flashes at the pictures when we were told of the importance of potatoes and carrots. Cartoons appeared in newspapers and magazines with messages from Potato Pete and Dr Carrot and there was a suggestion which quickly gained ground that carrots were good for the eyesight and the success of our night fighters was due to the fact that they ate quantities of carrots (years later we discovered it was radar). Some women were no longer throwing away their vegetable water, they were adding Oxo to it and making soup, just as the adverts from the Oxo company were telling them.

There was also Woolton Pie, a concoction of potatoes, carrots, parsnips and swedes topped with pastry. We gave it a try but decided it was horrible and I don't remember anyone having a good word for it.

In the summer margarine became rationed at four ounces a week and the butter ration was later cut to two ounces. That really hurt as Dad, who was working a three-shift system at British Celanese, took sandwiches every day and the butter or marge was being spread even more thinly.

But the worst was tea rationing which came in during July 1940 and was a miserable two ounces a week. We were great tea drinkers symbolised by the Boiling Kettle. As soon as you came into the house, the first thing you noticed was the kettle on the gas ring, quietly simmering away at all hours of the day, ever ready for the next 'mashing' (we never brewed or made tea, we always 'mashed').

'Who wants a cup of tea?' was the cry. The question seldom drew a negative. The heat was briefly turned up, the kettle boiled, three or four spoonfuls from the ancient pewter tea caddy placed in the earthenware teapot with rubber spout, the water poured on and in a few minutes we were having another round of cuppas.

But now that was under threat. As well as our tea drinking at home, Dad took tea to work in a small tin: he seemed to prefer making his own rather than canteen tea which he described as 'dishwater.' Now we had to come to terms with rationing although I detected the occasional extra two ounce packet found its way into the Langton household, as I was given the job of filling the caddy from the packets, being careful of course that every grain from the packet was deposited in the caddy.

We were now supplementing tea with other drinks such as cocoa, Ovaltine, Horlicks, Bovril, Oxo and Camp Coffee, although we were never enthusiastic coffee drinkers and it was regarded as some sort of a luxury. All the products were widely advertised during the war, each one setting out its beneficial effects, thus 'Fry's cocoa is packed with nourishment, energy and nerve strengthening substances', 'Bovril salutes the women of Britain and supplies them with a ready source of strength and energy that will help them through' and 'Mothers keep Horlicks for their children because of its energy-giving and body-building value .... mix it with water only.'

When the sugar ration was cut to eight ounces a week people started cutting it out altogether. That didn't appeal to me although I did daringly try a spoonful of golden syrup in my tea after hearing it was a good substitute but one mouthful was enough and I didn't repeat the experiment. However we did have syrup in porridge and this was palatable. In March of 1941 syrup along with jam and marmalade became rationed, followed by mincemeat, lemon curd and honey.

In May 1941 cheese went on ration at the measly amount of one ounce a week, just a good mouthful. We often had bread and cheese for supper and as my mother looked at the five ounce piece of cheese which was supposed to last the five of us a week (including sandwiches for Dad) she was lost for words. Miners and farm workers received extra, a generous eight ounces I think, resulting in a swop system ('We'll swop a pot of jam for two ounces of your cheese'). In fact some miners preferred jam to cheese. Later the cheese ration was increased to two ounces a week.

There was a great deal of jam making going on. The Government were encouraging this by allowing an extra sugar ration during the fruit season. Women's Institutes were renowned for their jam making and some organised their own fruit growing. My mother was not slow to join in. Like many of our neighbours we had a rhubarb patch and as soon as it was ready the rhubarb was boiling away on the gas ring. There was a great amount of stirring ('Here, stir this while I just nip up to Baileys. Keep stirring, don't stop'). Before long we had pots of the stuff with a home-made sticky label on the outside reading 'Rubarb Jam' (Mum's spelling was never of the highest order). Dad tried to avoid it but I think he sometimes found he had been caught when he opened his packed sandwiches at work. Tea time was often jam time when a large pot would appear on the table. Occasionally we were treated to a choice: plum jam.

In June 1941 came the announcement of egg rationing. The week before the scheme came in rumour swept Ilkeston that a Bath Street shop was selling unlimited quantities. There was a mass convergence on the premises where queues formed four deep all the way up the busy street. People were turning up with baskets and walking away with eggs filled to the brim. How such large stocks had been acquired was a mystery, particularly in view of the imminent rationing. Even the local paper posed the question: Can Lord Woolton explain these inconsistencies?

Egg rationing was a blow to us. My mother had a reputation for egg custard pies and scarcely a week went by without one appearing on the table, quickly devoured by the family. I often watched her making them, moulding the pastry in the deep enamel dish, followed by the egg and milk mixture that miraculously thickened into a creation which made her pies so scrumptious. Egg rationing meant an end to these treats.

She experimented with other cakes including an eggless family cake whose ingredients comprised 1 lb self-raising flour, 4 ounces margarine, 4 ounces sugar, 3 saccharin tablets, 14 ounces of currants, sultanas and peel, half pint of milk, half pint of water. Other cake recipes involved Dr Carrot and Potato

Pete (there was even carrot marmalade) but they often found their way to a neighbour's pig trough.

We also tried 'Frizettes' which my mother bought at Eaton & Woods, 'High Class Grocers' of Bath Street. A sixpenny packet made about thirty; only water had to be added to the powder before frying. They met with a mixed reception.

'What's this?' queried Dad suspiciously when a couple of Frizettes appeared on his plate. He seemed to doubt the claim of the manufacturer: 'You'll cease to worry about the egg shortage'.

Several neighbours in Richmond Avenue and 'over the wall' in Stratford Street kept hens and we were often wakened in the morning with the sound of a cock crowing. Occasionally hens would escape resulting in owners chasing through gardens ('Hey, mind my broad beans').

A popular song at the time went:

Hey little hen, when, when, when,

Will you lay me an egg for my tea,

Hey little hen, when, when, when,

Will you try to supply one for me.

Kitchen scraps to neighbours produced the occasional egg and the Elliott's next door kept a pig whose demise resulted in hunks of bacon.

In 1942 dried egg powder appeared from America. A tin contained the equivalent of a dozen eggs and an allowance of a tin a month per person was made in addition to the shell egg ration. Costing one shilling and sixpence a tin, the dried egg (to which water had to be added) was economical and popular.

Some foods, although not rationed, were very difficult to get. This particularly applied to fish and when supplies did arrive queues were legendary. People would queue for an hour or two for a piece of fish which was often of doubtful origin.

'My missus gen me a piece a fish I reckon had come out o' the cut' I once overheard on a bus.

'What did yer do, eat it or throw it back?' was the response.

When whalemeat or 'snoek' as it was termed arrived later in the war it was treated with the same suspicion as the man on the bus regarded his fish. It never became popular. Tripe was an alternative but not everyone had a taste for it. Sausages too were unrationed but you had to be at the butchers at the right time. Word soon spread when the butcher received his sausages which were variable in quality, many having a high bread content. It paid to be friendly with your local butcher and fishmonger. There were usually extra rations in December in time for Christmas.

December 1941 saw the introduction of the points rationing scheme in which every holder of a ration book received 16 points a month (later increased to 20) for tinned meat and fish and later for other items such as rice, tinned fruit, condensed milk, breakfast cereals and biscuits.

'Look, I've got a tin of corned beef and a tin of sardines from the Co-op' said my mother excitedly one day before Christmas. 'I've not had these for ages'. We hadn't. They had been 'under the counter' before points rationing, now they were suddenly appearing. Later in the war spam imported from America became a popular way of spending points. Some foods always seemed to be available however and I don't remember any shortages of bread, flour, custard powder, cocoa, pickles, sauces, Bovril or salt, although after the war bread became rationed.

As children, our biggest deprivations were sweets and chocolates. The pre-war displays of large glass bottles filled with tempting caramels, chocolate drops, mints, fruit drops and liquorish allsorts were almost non-existent and the ranges of chocolate bars were not to be seen, although if we were lucky we might find a few toffee bars, everlasting strips, sherbet dabs, 'kali' powder, aniseed balls, gobstoppers or cough sweets. Penny and twopenny bars of chocolate appeared briefly but you had to be around at the right time - if you saw a queue outside a sweet shop, you joined it. If you were extremely lucky you might get Mackintosh's Quality Street at eightpence a quarter or a twopence halfpenny packet of Rolo, assuming of course your pocket money stretched as far. Rationing was finally introduced in July 1942 by a 'personal points' scheme which allowed for eight ounces of confectionery for four weeks, later raised to twelve ounces.

Nearly every adult seemed to smoke during the war. We became used to smoke-filled buses, cinemas, canteens, restaurants, waiting rooms and air raid shelters, even the doctor in his surgery. Dad was on Craven A cork-tipped, Uncle Billy on Gold Flake, both heavy smokers. As the war went on, cigarettes became more difficult to get and smokers were prepared to take any brand although many drew the line at Pashas, a Turkish cigarette, which I had been told (erroneously) were made from camel dung. Popular brands became scarce in 1941 and queues built up outside tobacconists and newsagents. 'No Cigarettes' signs seemed to be permanently in place in some shops and once I heard a heated argument in a Bath Street newsagents when a potential customer accused the proprietor in very impolite language of having cigarettes under the counter for favoured customers only. I have never smoked and hate being near people who are smoking now but during the war we just accepted it, although I still remember the foul atmosphere of a crowded air raid shelter.

Beer also became short and from 1941 onwards 'No Beer' notices began appearing outside pubs. Ilkeston had a multitude of pubs and word soon got around which ones were open ('Trumpet's open tonight') but sometimes they opened later in the evening. Once I saw a neighbour setting off for the pub with a pint glass in his hand; apparently some pubs were short of glasses and encouraged customers to take their own. A common complaint was that some pubs were watering the beer and of course all drinkers complained about the price: it had risen from sixpence a pint pre-war to about elevenpence or a shilling due to Budget increases.

In the middle of the war the National Loaf appeared, made from flour of 85% extraction and said to be more nutritious than the white loaf. It was universally unpopular. 'Like eating cold pudding' I once heard.

Vegetables were not rationed and were usually fairly plentiful as many people took the Government's advice and cultivated an allotment as well as their own garden. DIG FOR VICTORY was one of the most famous slogans of the war which started only a month after the outbreak. We were told to dig up our lawns, uproot our flower beds and turn them over to growing vegetables. We were bombarded with leaflets and newspaper advertisements as well as posters on the cultivation of all types of vegetables. Our front garden which had delighted the eye with wallflowers, snapdragons and chrysanthemums was now sprouting cabbages, runner beans and onions.

Slogans such as HELP WIN THE WAR - WIELD THE SPADE - BEAT THE BLOCKADE appeared and full pages in the local papers were given over to the campaigns. People were urged to take an allotment and Ilkeston Corporation were advertising vegetable plants by the hundred or the score. 'Onions 1/6d per 100, cabbages 2d a score' was chalked on a notice in Victoria Park.

Gardening was not one of my interests in spite of my father's attempts to convert me and my heart sank when Hallcroft School acquired a piece of land near Oakwell for vegetable cultivation and we were taken by Mr Webster to clear the ground and plant the seed. On hearing this, my father joined in and I can see him now with spade and hoe, perspiration on his brow, digging for victory, while I and most of the other kids in the class were larking about.

Throughout the war of course you could still eat out in restaurants and although there was a maximum charge of five shillings a meal this sum would buy quite a substantial repast. The more expensive London restaurants even found ways round this, charging the maximum five shillings for a very elaborate meal but insisting you buy a drink at some extortionate figure.

Even the very wealthy however were having to come to terms with the situation. Just after the fall of France, Daily Mail columnist Charles Graves was writing 'There are naturally many repercussions of the French debacle. All kinds of French cheeses, vegetables, wines including Alsatian and most luxury goods will no longer be available to us.... Switzerland too is cut off so that Swiss cheeses, chocolate and various other commodities are difficult to obtain.'

What a beastly war it was becoming for the rich. The same columnist on 7 August 1940 was lamenting that champagne was already more or less sold out and stocks would be exhausted by the end of September, brandy by the end of the current month and kummel was already sold out. (I never came across any kummel drinkers in Ilkeston and I doubt if one in a hundred would have recognised this German liqueur if they had tasted it).

'So it looks as though we shall all be back to our traditional drinks - whisky, beer, cider, gin and homemade wines. All of which is going to make life very difficult for Harry of Harry's Bar who is about to start a snack counter at the Ritz hotel.'

Poor Harry.

Eighteen months into the war, Ilkeston had its first British Restaurant where hot mid-day meals were served at moderate prices. Situated in Station Road, it proved to be a great success from the word go. On its opening day in May 1941 queues formed well before noon and the food soon ran out. People were not just sitting in to eat, some were arriving with basins to take the food away. Food controllers had to be approached to increase the food allocation.

I noted in my wartime diary that a second British Restaurant opened on 3 July 1941 at the Dicona premises on Heanor Road which was more convenient to us and I sometimes used this on Saturdays or school holidays. On the opening day 300 adults and 200 children crowded in and it was nearly always busy when I went.

The British Restaurants were a new experience. On my first visit I had to get used to the system: pick up a tray and go to the meat counter where one of the ladies ladled the soup into a bowl and another placed a small portion of meat or a rissole on a plate and heaped it up with generous portions of potatoes, cabbage and swede. You moved on to pay at the little window (soup a penny, meat course sixpence). You then took your tray to one of the long wooden tables where diners were seated on chairs or long forms (I always tried to get a chair). Very often we found ourselves sitting shoulder to shoulder. There was also a sweet course available for twopence at another serving counter such as jam roly-poly or spotted dick buried under a mound of custard, or if you were unlucky, there were prunes. The lot could be washed down with a lukewarm cup of tea for another penny. By the end of the war there were 2,000 British Restaurants in the country serving half a million meals a day.

Rationing and food shortages also led to court cases. In March 1941 two butchers were fined £25 each for supplying excess meat to Stanton Ironworks canteen while the supervisor at Stanton was fined £40 for contravening regulations.

Charnos were in hot water in December 1940 when it was discovered that they had been supplied with tea rations for ninety people whereas in fact only 36 employees had been provided with tea. The summons was brought under a section of the Rationing Order 1939 which stipulated that for every twenty persons one pound of tea in weight per month would be supplied. It was stated in court that Charnos had received four and a half pounds of tea, sufficient for ninety employees, their total workforce, whereas only male employees were provided with tea which sounds like discrimination and a throw back to the dark ages. In dismissing the case the chairman of the magistrates said 'We dismiss the case but at the same time we do not want you to think that an offence has not been committed, but we believe that it has not been done wilfully.' The firm were ordered to pay eighteen shillings costs and two guineas advocate's fee.

In another case a Granby Street greengrocer was fined £5 for imposing a condition of sale. Apparently he told a woman customer he would not sell her a pound of potatoes unless she bought sixpence worth of spring onions. A woman at Heanor was fined £2 for using a ration book wrongfully: the book belonged to an evacuee who had returned home.

Although the Ministry of Food were employing nearly a thousand inspectors only a relatively small number of offenders were being prosecuted. A few strange cases appeared in court including one of a lady prosecuted for permitting bread to be wasted: she had been caught feeding birds during the winter. There was a thriving black market and if you had money you could get almost anything. Shopkeepers usually had the odd tin of salmon and other goodies for their better off customers and there were always spivs who could supply food, clothing, petrol and tyres at a price.

However, rationing and price controls made for a fairer distribution. Working people were earning good money and the pre-war 'distressed areas' had disappeared, in fact many people were eating better than ever before, even though the diet may have been monotonous.

52

CHAPTER SIX
BACKS TO THE WALL

My war diary had been growing. There was not much excitement on what we called the Home Front but there was action in other parts of Europe. I had recorded 'Russia invades Finland' on the last day of November 1939. After Christmas it looked as if the Russians were winning and there was a lot of talk about helping the poor Finns. However by March the Finns had been beaten and signed a peace treaty with the Russians.

Next came Denmark and Norway which were invaded by the Germans on 9 April 1940 according to my diary to which I added 'main ports seized'. Denmark soon surrendered - they didn't seem to have much of an army - but Norway defended well. Then our naval forces went in and we were told British troops had landed. We began hearing new names, Narvik, Namsos, Trondheim, Stavanger and Bergen which I was able to find on my large scale war map of Europe. When we captured Narvik I stuck a small Union Jack on the place, then we heard our troops were 'resisting enemy pressure' and in May I had to remove the Union Jack when we withdrew.

People were becoming very critical. My uncle, in his no-nonsense manner, was blaming the Government. He had fought in the First World War in the Royal Artillery - a 'real war' he called it - but the present war was just a phoney, nothing much was happening, and whatever we did, we made a mess of it.

'We've just got kicked out of Norway, the U-boats are sinking our ships, our troops are sitting on their behinds on the Maginot Line, we're groping about in the bloody blackout, fined if we shine a light and you can't get a decent meal, everybody's browned off. What's the Government doing? Nowt except make more paperwork and set on more clerks.'

I had heard him before chuntering about the Government and civil servants. We listened to Tommy Handley, the comedian, in his radio show ITMA ('It's That Man Again'), who poked fun at officials in the 'Ministry of Aggravation' (his way of combining Agriculture and Information) and the 'Office of Twerps' (Works). So much paper work had been created because of the hundreds of new regulations and rationing 'nobody can find time to fight a war' said Uncle Billy. It all seemed very puzzling.

I heard the wife of a soldier say that she only got seventeen shillings a week and ten bob for her three children. 'I can't make ends meet on that, my parents have to help me, don't know what I'd do without them. While my husband's in the army, other chaps in reserved occupations are earning big money, five or six pounds a week and more.'

People were generally complaining that the well-off were doing very nicely while others such as servicemen's families, old age pensioners and those doing menial jobs were badly off. Local people were also complaining there was nothing in the shops to buy and what used to be the popular Ilkeston market wasn't worth going to any more. 'Just two or three tinpot stalls' was a comment which just about summed it up, in fact the Town Council debated whether to turn the Market Place into a public park.

A row developed in the local Labour Party after a report appeared in the Ilkeston Advertiser of 15 December 1939 that a special conference called by the Ilkeston Borough Labour Party and Trades Council recorded striking unanimity that 'the war was imperialist and against the interest of the working class' and a resolution denouncing it and calling for opposition to the National Government was unanimously carried. One speaker said the Labour Party was blindly following its leaders, Attlee, Greenwood and Dalton, but the rank and file should not follow as there was nothing in the war for the workers.

This drew an angry reply from a local Labour official, Councillor Hoult, saying the Labour Party had a few Communists amongst its ranks who did not represent the opinions of the great majority who supported the war, as did George Oliver, the local Labour Member of Parliament.

Oliver had won the seat in 1935 and could be relied on to follow the party line. One of our neighbours attended the traditional May Day meeting in the Market Place where Mr Oliver addressed a crowd of two or three hundred people (how many would attend such a meeting today?).

In his speech George Oliver said Labour stood for collective security and he was against those left wingers who wanted to call the war off adding 'In that point of view I think there is an element of treachery.' The situation was now grave and events in Norway were not to be looked upon with joy but he did not think Italy would come into the war (how wrong he was). A rival demonstration organised by the Communist Party attacked Labour leaders who supported the war as this meant wage cuts, they contended.

Many Ilkeston families had been affected by the call-up or as the Ilkeston Advertiser poetically put it in May 1940: 'There are 1500 of the flower of Ilkeston manhood now serving in H.M. Forces.' Some were in northern

France with the BEF, some were on the high seas combating the U boat threat, others were in the RAF. One of these was Tim Newcombe, who lived next door to us with his parents and sister. We had known him a couple of years since moving to Richmond Avenue, quietly spoken and well liked, always with a cheerful word. At the age of 21 he had been called up for the RAF and was serving on a Suffolk aerodrome when he met with an accident, killing him instantly. The death of someone we knew so well cast a dark cloud over the whole neighbourhood.

The war situation was now taking a critical turn. Following our withdrawal from Norway the news bulletins were saying that Parliament was debating the conduct of the war. Uncle Billy was quite sure what should happen: Chamberlain should go. He was right. After the debate he handed in his resignation.

'Winston Churchill becomes Prime Minister' was my diary entry for 10 May 1940 followed by 'Hitler invades Belgium and Holland.' The Panzas swept through the two countries like a knife through butter, seven divisions of them, 1800 tanks supported by dive bombers. It was called Blitzkrieg. They burst through into Northern France; the armies of Holland, Belgium, France and the British Expeditionary Force could not hold them. The impregnable Maginot Line was well to the south and useless to the Allies. Huge numbers of French and British troops were trapped as the well-equipped Germans reached the Channel coast.

Churchill's priority was to get our troops back home. It was then that we began to hear the name Dunkirk and we saw pictures in the papers of men on the beaches waiting for ships to bring them back - naval ships, fishing boats, paddle steamers, every type of vessel that could cross the Channel. It was called Operation Dynamo. Altogether 338,000 troops were brought back, 225,000 of them were British. 'A miracle' the papers were saying, but there was no escaping the fact that the Germans had won a great victory and they were now facing us across the Channel, just twenty odd miles away. The swastika was flying from the Eiffel Tower and Italy came into the war against us.

The barbed wire was going up along our beaches. The enemy could invade at any time. We were issued with a leaflet 'If the Invader Comes' which said 'Think always of your country before you think of yourself.' We were told that if the invaders came church bells would be rung and we were ordered to 'Stay Put.' This advice was given after the experience in France when civilians clogged the roads fleeing from the Germans making it impossible for the army to move.

On 18 June we sat by the wireless to hear Churchill make one of his famous broadcasts: 'The battle of France is over. I expect that the Battle of Britain is about to begin .... let us therefore brace ourselves to our duties, and so bear ourselves that, if the British Empire and its Commonwealth last for a thousand years, men will still say: This was their finest hour.'

Suddenly things had changed. Boredom and indifference had gone. We had a purpose. We were now alone.

'Thank God' said a neighbour. 'We're better off without the French.' Even the King had written in a letter 'Personally I feel happier that we have no allies to be polite to.'

The adrenaline was flowing and we called it the Dunkirk Spirit. Churchill's epic speeches were a rallying point; each speech was listened to with rapt attention. After the nine o'clock news on Sunday evenings we also listened to the fifteen minute broadcasts of J.B. Priestley, a blunt speaking pipe smoking Yorkshireman who always made us feel good, no matter how bad the news was. Just after the retreat from Dunkirk he talked about the little boats which brought many of the troops back:

'Among the paddle steamers that will never return was one that I knew well - none other than the good ship "Gracie Fields", for she was the glittering queen of our local line, and instead of taking an hour over her voyage, used to do it, churning like mad, in forty five minutes. And now never again will we board her at Cowes .... she has paddled and churned away for ever. But now this little steamer, like all her brave and battered sisters, is immortal. She'll go sailing down the years in the epic of Dunkirk. And our great grandchildren, when they learn how we began this war by snatching glory out of defeat and then swept on to victory, may also learn how the little holiday steamers made an excursion to hell and came back glorious.'

You could not help but feel better after hearing that.

The country had to be defended and even before Dunkirk the War Secretary, Anthony Eden, had made an appeal for civilians to come forward and form a new force which he called the Local Defence Volunteers or LDV for short. As soon as it was announced, volunteers were arriving at local police stations to enrol. In Ilkeston at the beginning of June, Major F. Robinson who was commanding 'B' company soon had enough men to form several platoons, in fact the response had been so good there was a waiting list.

The anti-invasion force, was renamed Home Guard, maybe because Local Defence Volunteers was a bit of a mouthful or maybe because its initials had been translated as 'Look, Duck and Vanish.' It was for British subjects between the ages of 17 and 65, part-time unpaid, although a free uniform was provided. A quarter of a million men enlisted immediately and at first neither uniforms nor weapons were available and the first pictures in the papers showed an amateurish looking army, most still in civvies and one rifle between about twenty men. Cartoons were soon appearing of Home Guards armed with bows and arrows and swords.

Their duties were to set up observation posts, guard power stations, gasworks and railways, set up night patrols, road blocks and deal with enemy parachutists. Retired army officers or local business men were often put in charge of units, especially those who owned a car. The Territorial Associations often helped to select them and this led to complaints that 'Colonel Blimps' were running the show with too much emphasis on square bashing and boot polishing rather than modern battle tactics.

I was in Shipley Woods one day with a friend when we heard noises off the main path. We approached gingerly and as we came to a clearing we saw an

56

elderly man in soldier's uniform sitting on the grass blindfolded holding a stick in his hand which I supposed was meant to be a gun. From behind trees on the far side of the clearing were men silently creeping forward, obviously to avoid detection. They took it in turn to approach the blindfolded man and when they were close enough, snatched his stick giving a whoop of triumph. Not all were successful however, some being detected before they had time to snatch the stick when the target threw off his blindfold, pointed his stick and shouted 'bang.' We were quite enjoying this until one of them spotted us when we were angrily told to clear off.

One of the main tasks of the Home Guard was to watch for enemy parachutists although the Air Ministry had to remind people that not all parachutists were enemies after some of our own pilots baling out had been shot at. The most famous case was that of Flt Lt James Nicolson, the only fighter pilot to win the VC, who baled out over Hampshire after a dogfight, only to be fired at and wounded by a Home Guard.

We heard that the Germans had dropped parachutists in France and the Low Countries disguised as nuns or in uniforms of the allies (all untrue, no doubt) so that we could expect the enemy to be dropped amongst us in disguise, perhaps even as miners. Any suspicious groups should be challenged which sounded all very well in theory but there were practical difficulties. We came to the conclusion that challenging a group of miners walking along Cotmanhay Road would be a risky business and the Government's advice to stop them and demand to see their identity cards did not appeal. If they were real Germans we would probably finish up as target practice, if they were real miners it would be 'Bogger off before I bat yer tab.'

Of course it was much better to report your suspicions to the police or the military and consequently they were inundated with reports from well-meaning citizens of suspicious persons and their activities. Our imaginations were working overtime as we looked at strangers in a new light.

'Look at him with a beard and hat pulled over his eyes, I reckon he's a Jerry.'

'Don't be daft, he's a teacher at Bennerley.'

We were also listening for foreign or unusual accents ('Vich is der vay to Vhatstandvell Vatervorks?') which was bad luck for the Irish, Scots and Geordies, let alone the thousands of Free French, Poles, Czechs and Empire service men in the country.

On 31 May orders were given to remove all signposts which were taken down throughout the country and not put back until autumn 1942 in urban areas and mid-1943 in rural areas. Mileposts were uprooted, names of streets, railway stations and village names were painted out. This certainly made life difficult for the British and many people got lost outside their own locality. Travelling by train became a nightmare and there were numerous instances of passengers travelling beyond their destinations ('Is this Kimberley?' 'No duck, that was two stations back, this is Ilkeston')

For some months there had been disquiet about the powers of the Home Guard. The police were not happy at the amount of power of search and arrest which the Home Guard had been given. People out and about at night were constantly being stopped, asked for identity cards and, if these could not be produced, taken to the nearest police station. Courting couples were often the targets of zealous Home Guards. Even policemen were stopped and asked to produce their warrant cards, some challenged at gunpoint while high-ranking army officers were stopped in their staff cars.

Even worse there appeared to be a gung-ho attitude amongst some Home Guards. General Ironside, the C-in-C, declared in June 1940 'If the intruder is a spy or an enemy you are entitled to shoot him .... the gentlemen who are best behaved are those doing the mischief. We cannot be too sure of anybody'.

A 'shoot first, ask questions afterwards' policy occurred in some cases, especially at road blocks which the Home Guard set up at nights. In pitch darkness these were not easily seen with screened headlights or not acted on in time. On one night in June 1940 four motorists were shot and killed in various parts of the country and there were a number of other cases including one at Ilkeston in September 1940 when Mr George Locker who was employed at Ilkeston LNER was challenged by a Home Guard sentry. Mr Locker, who was deaf, failed to hear the challenge and was promptly shot dead in his car. The irony was that he was a platoon commander in the Home Guard.

The setting up of road blocks sometimes caused problems when civil defence workers in emergencies were held up and there were cases of fire engines during the blitz being delayed. Pressure was put on the Home Guard to restrain their ardour. Gradually battalions were being equipped with khaki battledress, some even had great coats and steel helmets. Shotguns and pistols which had been handed in by the public were issued to Home Guards and a few were given Lee Enfield rifles. Other weapons included home made Molotov cocktails and even an anti-tank gun was recorded.

And then there were the pikes, one of the biggest jokes of the war. These were long metal tubes with a bayonet blade welded into the end. When we first saw the Home Guards on parade with some of them holding these unwieldy monstrosities we just laughed. They too were very self conscious of them and they soon disappeared, probably confined to stores.

We may have laughed at the pikes but there was not much else to laugh about. The situation was grim and evacuation was back on the agenda, reminding me that at the beginning of the war I had written in my diary: '1,300,000 evacuated in 4,000 special trains in four days.' From London and the big cities, the vast numbers of children had been moved into the country or 'reception areas' as they were known. Many of them had gone back home when air raids failed to materialise and parents were asked to contribute to their children's upkeep. But now they were being evacuated again, some of them to Derbyshire. This time, however, it was better organised - the first evacuation which had taken place at short notice was chaotic with children being dumped in towns and villages and no definite homes to go to, resulting in scenes something like a cattle market.

On Sunday 2 June 1940 trains brought three thousand evacuees to Derbyshire from the Southend area of Essex. A local newspaper reported 'After being passed by the medical officer as they waited on the platforms the children were taken to private buses waiting outside the station and then conveyed to the distributing centres before being taken to their new homes.' Belper received 1,600, Ripley 500 and Ashbourne 800. None came to Ilkeston which was a 'neutral' area at the time but nearby villages took some of the evacuees including 40 at Mapperley village, 63 at Smalley, 50 at Kilburn, 50 at Horsley Woodhouse and 27 at Horsley. Settling in had its problems and the people of Mapperley were not pleased when they read a local newspaper report that a ten year old evacuee had said the villagers spoke 'a kind of broken English' (Ey up mi duck?) and an eight year old announced that 'Mapperley has some slums but they are a bit better than London.'

A year later twenty of the evacuees were suddenly removed from their foster parents at Mapperley on the instructions of Belper RDC. The Ilkeston Advertiser of 6 June 1941 reported: 'This decision followed the exposure of most unfortunate circumstances which made it eminently desirable to remove all children billeted at Mapperley. It is not possible to give details of the affair in these columns but in announcing that children were being sent to other parishes in the area Mr G.A. Dawes, Chief Billeting Officer for Belper RDC stated "We are concerned with the welfare of the children and it is only their interests we are thinking of in this case. The decision to remove the children has been agreed upon by the Chief Officer of Education for Southend, the police authorities and myself. Their movement should not for a single moment be regarded as any reflection upon any foster parent in Mapperley. Foster parents are warmly thanked for all the voluntary efforts they have made in the interests of the children during the past year."' Clearly the problem lay at the school.

A few Ilkeston families became interested in a new Government scheme to send their children overseas. The Dominions and the United States offered to take British children now that the situation was grave. British parents had to decide between the risks of keeping their children with the threat of invasion and bombing or whether to send them overseas with the risk of evacuee ships being torpedoed. About 200,000 applications were received including 106 from Ilkeston. By September only 2,700 had been evacuated although 11,000 others had been sent privately by the better off who could afford the passage. The scheme came to a tragic end when the City of Benares was torpedoed with the loss of 73 children.

In November 1940 forty families who had been bombed out in London consisting of 120 people, mostly women and children, arrived in Ilkeston 'bleary-eyed and weak and almost exhausted through lack of sleep but with unbroken spirit.' The majority had been evacuated under the official Government scheme and billeted with relatives or friends in the district.

Some had obtained tenancies of houses, some had brought their own furniture and some of the men found work in the town while one had become an air raid warden. It would be interesting to know how many of these settled permanently in the district.

Because of a fear that a German invasion might result in the capture of the BBC and broadcasting services, newsreaders began announcing their names before each bulletin ('This is the one o'clock news and this is Bruce Belfrage/Frank Phillips/Alvar Liddell reading it').

With the possibility that we had spies in our midst the Ministry of Information ran anti-gossip campaigns resulting in a series of posters, some of them comic, the most famous of which was CARELESS TALK COSTS LIVES drawn by the artist Kenneth Bird under the name Fougasse. One showed Hitler and Goering sitting behind two gossiping women with the caption 'You never know who's listening'. Another one showed a man and a woman at a dinner table, one saying 'Of course there's no harm in your knowing' while Hitler crouched under the table with a notebook.

Other posters urged us to 'Be like Dad, keep Mum' (that would not be allowed today) and 'Keep it under your hat'. The posters made a big impact with people often repeating the catch phrases which were more effective than some of the staid advertisements such as a rather rambling '...The country asks you to join the Silent Column, the great body of sensible people who when not to talk and who will, in the event of an invasion, stop the rumours that lead to confusion...' and so on at some length.

The newspapers were subject to voluntary censorship. The Ministry of Information had been created at the outbreak of war and part of its duties was to vet articles and reports submitted by newspapers which might contain information valuable to the enemy.

Defence notices were issued to all editors which listed subjects on which no information should be published without advice from the censor, and editors also received scores of memos on banned topics.

During the blitz the press were only allowed to name bombed cities when it was obvious and the Germans knew which city they had targeted, but little or no detail was given such as specific localities, factories or buildings, although these were sometimes given at a much later date, presumably to confuse the enemy.

When Ilkeston was bombed on the night of 30 August 1940 it resulted in a front page story in the Ilkeston Advertiser of 6 September headlined RAIDERS VISIT THE MIDLANDS. This stated that 'German raiders which visited a Midlands town on Friday night dropped more than 50 incendiary bombs on the outskirts of a residential area'. Little detail was given and the report added that firemen who put out the incendiaries were 'as keen as mustard' and 'there was absolutely no panic of any kind and the morale of even the oldest people was very good'.

I would imagine that everyone who read that report would have known that the Midlands town was Ilkeston but of course the editor of the Advertiser decided under the guide lines that the name of the town should be witheld and there was certainly no reference to the nearby Charnos factory or Stanton Ironworks, both of which escaped damage.

This voluntary system was backed by legal sanctions under which it was an offence for anyone to publish or convey to the enemy information that would assist him. First, the Ministry had to warn the newspaper concerned and if this was disregarded a prosecution would follow.

Another regulation could be used to close down a newspaper if it was fomenting opposition to the war. In fact the Daily Worker was closed down in January 1941. The Government also threatened with closure the Daily Mirror and the Sunday Pictorial after articles appeared criticising the conduct of the Government but no action was taken as it was felt important to uphold the principles of democracy and freedom of expression, after all that is what we were supposed to be fighting for.

The newspapers were seriously reduced in size. In 1940 the popular papers were down to eight pages but later in the war they produced issues of only four pages and the sports pages were almost abolished although space was always made available for racing. Nearly every working man including my father and many women liked a daily bet on the horses.

When my father was on the afternoon or night shift he spent part of his mornings studying Templegate in the Daily Herald and the 'nap' selection was often incorporated into a series of doubles and a treble.

On Wednesdays the papers published the football coupon. The various companies - Littlewoods, Vernons, Copes, Shermans, Socapools, Bonds, Jervis and Screen - had merged into one Unity Pool. My father would study this at some length, occasionally asking my opinion ('What do you think of Mansfield v Notts?). He would be deciding whether to go for the Penny Points Pool demanding 14 selections and paying four dividends with the chance of a big win ('think I'll have twelve lines for a bob this week') and how to 'invest' another shilling (three draws, four aways or Easy Six - the latter was a complete misnomer as it had the most difficult matches to forecast on the coupon). Usually it was a few entries on each, probably amounting to two shillings or half a crown. The coupon was filled in and the postal order purchased for the previous week's bets as betting in those days was strictly on a credit basis and you always paid after the results were known. Ready money betting was illegal for pools and horse racing.

The papers at the time often carried reports of men coming before tribunals to be registered as Conscientious Objectors. Some were granted, others were not. Usually the objections were on religious or humanitarian grounds, but in January 1940 the Ilkeston Advertiser reported that a man who claimed he was a life-long vegetarian was not allowed to be included on the CO register. In July 1940 Ilkeston Town Council passed a resolution to take immediate steps to terminate the engagement of any employee who had applied to be placed on the CO register. Derbyshire County Council also decided to dismiss all employees who were registered COs after two had registered. Nottinghamshire County Council on the other hand decided that any registered COs in its employ would in future receive the same wages as a private in the army, a huge reduction and probably making it impossible for them to carry on working for the County Council.

Derby bus drivers and conductors evidently felt very strongly on the matter. A petition was organised signed by 230 employees in the omnibus department and presented to the Committee calling on them to sack a conductor who had been exempted from war service on religious grounds. The Committee referred the matter to the Special Purposes Committee who decided that the government take them from their present employment and find them some other work of national importance. When the matter came before the full council it was decided to give leave of absence without pay for the period of hostilities to all COs employed by the Corporation.

Back in Ilkeston, arguments were raging over this thorny question. At the October meeting of Ilkeston Town Council Alderman Shaw, the chairman, said pressure had been brought to bear on the Council by the Free Church Council to alter their previous resolution dismissing employees who were COs. He personally thought they were COs if they joined non-combative units and added: 'If they are real COs they would refuse to eat food brought across the seas by our fighting forces and if they carried this out they would die!'

Councillor Hoult said 99% of ratepayers had no use for COs. He thought they should be given the dangerous but life-saving job of dealing with unexploded bombs. Mrs McIntyre said she had admiration for real COs but some people took advantage of the law to 'slide through'. She personally knew a CO who was doing minesweeping duties. Another councillor said that what he objected to were 'plenty of people who slipped out of the forces', not because they were COs but because they were supposed to be on work of national importance. He believed that the Churches should stand up and back courageous men and women who stood by their principles. Another councillor thought that the young man who had been sacked by Ilkeston Council was the victim of a tactical mistake.

After a lengthy debate the Council agreed to delete their previous resolution and substituting it for one that COs would be dismissed unless they undertook non-combative duties in the Forces, in other words they could have their jobs back at the end of the war.

During the war 59,000 claimed objection and of these 3,500 were given unconditional exemption, 28,700 were registered on condition they took up approved work (generally in agriculture or staying in their present jobs), 14,700 were registered for non-combative duties in the armed forces and 12,200 were turned down. A few went to jail for their principles, unlike the first World War when over 6,000 (out of a total of 16,000 objectors) went to prison. Feelings against COs were never as strong during the Second World War except for a period during 1940 when we had our 'backs to the wall'. Even so, Ernest Bevin, Minister of Labour, made a speech in the House of Commons in July 1940 deprecating most strongly any victimisation of COs. It is interesting to note that during the first World War Herbert Morrison, a member of Churchill's cabinet, was a CO.

What do I do...

to help in Britain's campaign for SALVAGE?

I tie into bundles all PAPER and CARDBOARD, including books, old magazines, office records, catalogues, correspondence, music, wallpaper ends, etc., which are no longer of value.

I save METAL, including tins, washing them clean and pressing them flat.

I save BONES, keeping them clean and dry.

I return EMPTY BOTTLES to the shops from which they came, or give them, along with the other salvage, to the dustman.

Cut this out—and keep it!

Issued by the Ministry of Information

Space presented to the Nation by the Brewers' Society

→→→ THE ←←←
CHOCOLATE CODE

I **won't** try to buy chocolate in all the shops I pass. I'll ration myself of my own free will.

I **won't** eat chocolate just for pleasure. I'll leave it for the children. I know that it's an important food for them, and a rare treat as well.

I **won't** try to get more chocolate than I used to eat in peace-time. I'll make up with other foods not so scarce.

I **won't** blame the shopkeeper if he can't serve me with chocolate. I know he's doing his best.

I'll **only** eat chocolate to give me energy for hard work that is helping on the war effort.

63

CHAPTER SEVEN
SAUCEPANS INTO SPITFIRES

'It's a Spitfire.'

'No it's not, it's a Hurricane.'

'Betcha.'

'Betcha last week's Knock Out comic for your Dandy.'

'O.K.'

As the plane hurtled closer the familiar lines of the Spitfire with its more graciously curved wings became apparent. I had won a comic.

We were all keen aeroplane spotters. The papers printed pictures of British and German aircraft and there were also identification charts - I had one on my bedroom wall - showing three or four silhouettes of each aircraft. I had studied the lines of the Spitfire, Hurricane, Blenheim, Hampden and Wellington as well as the German planes, the Heinkel He 111k, the Dornier Do 17, the Junkers Ju 87 (the screaming dive bomber!) and Ju 88 and the Messerschmitt Me 109. I had not seen any German planes in the first few months of war but I thought I knew what to look out for. We were also told that they made a heavy droning sound, quite different to ours.

Spitfires were seldom seen over Ilkeston; they were mainly based in the south of England where the action was expected to take place. We had to be content with the more mundane training planes based at the nearby Hucknall aerodrome. Occasionally I borrowed Dad's bike and cycled the six miles where I took up a position in a field adjoining the airfield, being careful of course to keep a low profile as I didn't want to be arrested as a Nazi spy. Everybody was on the lookout for spies who could be disguised as anybody, perhaps even someone wearing a Hallcroft school cap. But I was never challenged and spent an hour or two watching the little Tiger

Moth biplanes taking off with their trainee pilots and instructors performing various manoeuvres and landings of varying quality. I also saw the larger monoplanes such as the Fairey Battle and an occasional Hurricane.

Hucknall had been operating since the First World War and in 1936 the RAF moved in with numbers 98 and 104 Squadrons with bombers, Hawker Horsleys and Hinds and Westland Wallaces. It changed briefly to Fighter Command with Hurricanes but by 1940 it had become a Polish training unit. The Poles remained there for the duration of the war.

There was excitement one day in 1940 when an escaped German prisoner tried to steal a plane to fly back to Germany. He turned up at Hucknall saying he was a Dutch pilot and wanted to fly back to his base. His story sounded plausible and a plane was made ready for him but in the nick of time he was rumbled and arrested.

We started to hear a lot about the Ministry of Aircraft Production which had a new boss, Lord Beaverbrook, who gave absolute priority to producing new planes, almost at the expense of everything else. Monthly production figures of fighters shot up from 256 in April 1940 to a peak of 496 in July. Lord Beaverbrook's photo began appearing everywhere, especially the Daily Express of which he was the proprietor.

'I want your pots and pans' he told us. 'We will turn them into Spitfires, Hurricanes, Blenheims and Wellingtons.' People were handing in their old saucepans, frying pans and kettles.

'Well loaded lorries containing old iron have been reported in the Borough' stated the Ilkeston Advertiser on 28 June 1940. A few weeks later half a ton of scrap aluminium, mainly in the form of pots and pans, had been deposited at the Rutland Hotel, headquarters of the Women's Voluntary Service who had organised the collection. We were being assailed on all sides to turn out salvage which was being collected by the WVS.

'Separate your salvage' we were told. People were throwing out all manner of things and although much of it was junk, some worthwhile items did emerge.

'My eyes are too bad to do much reading now. In any case I could do with the room' said an elderly neighbour pointing to a great pile of books near her back door when a WVS lady called.

'Oh I think they're too good for salvage' she said looking at the impressive volumes of Dickens, Hardy and Thackeray. I'll see they go to the Forces. They badly need books.'

We turned out old magazines and comics (what would a present day collector give for the old Beanos and Dandies!) and a kettle with a hole in it.

Then Lord Beaverbrook came up with another idea, the Spitfire Fund. Spitfires were said to cost £5,000 so towns and villages began opening funds and soon practically every fair sized town in the country had its name on a Spitfire. Ilkeston opened its own fund in October 1940. A large banner appeared outside the public library A SPITFIRE A DAY KEEPS JERRY AWAY. All kinds of money-raising schemes were mooted and collecting tins were being rattled everywhere, in shops, businesses and at various events. We even had a house to house collection. Two local hairdressers, Miss P. Hallam and Mr H.M. Abbott, each ran raffles for a free permanent wave, the library organised a competition, Greaves Furnishers raised money by displaying a model convoy, someone gave a gold watch, a number of ladies were making and selling pin cushions, iron holders and other small articles while Spitfire badges were selling well at sixpence each.

Popular with the male half of the town was a model aircraft and engineering exhibition which I attended with my young brother. We joined the queue for an exciting ride on a one-eighth scale model of the famous GWR steam locomotive King George V. There were some impressive model aircraft to admire but I am afraid that's as far as it went with me: I never could get enthusiastic about actually making the models.

I had discovered this when I had been given a balsa wood kit as a birthday present. It languished in its box for some time before my parents goaded me into cutting and gluing the pieces ('we spent good money on that'). When it did not seem to be working out, they insisted on paying one of my school friends, a keen modeller, the sum of sixpence to finish it. He made quite a professional job and painted it in camouflage. Dad and I tried it out on Bennerley Rec and it actually flew, the propeller whirring away as the elastic ran down. However I could not work up sufficient enthusiasm for it and it was soon relegated to the spare room.

The highlight of the Spitfire Fund campaign was the exhibit of a Messerschmitt 109 which had been brought down during a raid 'somewhere in England' we were told. It was on view at the premises of a removal firm, William ('Billy') West's and was one of the fearsome-looking 'yellow nose' squadron. There were large queues to see the Luftwaffe's most lethal fighter plane and the admission charge of sixpence (children threepence) was pronounced to be a bargain and raised £180 for the fund.

In spite of the popularity of this and other events, the Spitfire Fund was becoming something of an embarrassment for Ilkeston. The target of £5,000 which had been set was clearly far too ambitious as only about £1,200 had been raised by the end of 1940. It was then decided to organise an auction sale and householders were asked to turn out their cupboards, drawers and attics.

When the organisers appealed for good quality items of value I don't think they expected a Shetland pony but that is what they got from Mr G.W. Spendlove. The idea was to parade the animal round the town on a fund-raising trip, then auction it. The pony however had different ideas, thwarting attempts to catch and decorate him. Various suggestions were made to the Spitfire Committee including staging a rodeo and awarding a prize to the first person who could catch and handle the perverse animal. An SOS was given out: Anybody who knows anything about horses is asked to get in touch with the Committee. This proved to be good pub conversation material for days ('Ah reckon ah could ride 'im', 'yo' couldna ride a clothes 'oss').

Billy the pony was put in Corporation stables waiting to do his bit for the war effort but in the meantime costing £10 for his feed and care. Eventually, he was tamed and decorated and paraded round the town one Saturday in February by Mr P. Riley who apparently had a way with animals. Billy was stroked and admired and raised two pounds two shillings and elevenpence for the fund. This was deemed a success and further forays into the town raised the total to £15.

A Sunday concert in aid of the fund ran into trouble with religious bodies and some members of the Town Council. It was not just the fact of being held on a Sunday, it was the content of the show which drew criticism. Local Methodists described it as of a 'highly secular nature' while a councillor conceded that 'there is no doubt that one artiste was disgraceful' and he did not think they should get a reputation for holding 'dirty concerts'.

The auction sale took place on Easter Monday 1941 having attracted over a thousand lots. £205 was raised including 25 guineas for Billy the pony. This brought the fund total to £2,060, less than half the cost of a Spitfire.

However it has to be said that so many appeals were being made in the town during this time that it was hardly surprising. There seemed to be flag days almost every Saturday for a whole range of forces charities, appeals for Ilkeston hospital and many comforts funds organised by firms, clubs and pubs. I once heard a man remark that he had stopped going into the Hand and Heart at Cotmanhay as he thought he had given as much to their Troop Fund as he had paid out for beer.

During the summer of 1940 nearly all the action was taking place in the south of England; living in the Midlands we could only read or listen to reports on the wireless, or at least what the Ministry of Information allowed. We turned on the wireless one day in July 1940 to hear a vivid account by BBC commentator Charles Gardner of an aerial combat which was taking place over Dover. He just happened to be there when RAF fighters were attacking a Junkers 87 and we heard him saying 'He's coming down in flames completely out of control .... a long streak of smoke, the pilot's baled out by parachute .... he's going slap into the sea .... there he goes .... smash .... the RAF fighters have really got these boys taped.'

Exciting stuff. The dogfights in the air were copied in the playgrounds. New games were invented. Younger boys were chasing around, arms outstretched, ducking and diving and machine-gunning each other. The only problem was that everyone wanted to be either a Spitfire or a Hurricane, nobody wanted to be a Messerschmitt or a Heinkel.

Suddenly there were lots of entries in my war diary:

8 August: 60 German planes shot down in aerial battles over the Channel after attacking our convoys .... large numbers of Ju 87 dive-bombers escorted by Messerschmitts .... 16 British fighter pilots missing, three later rescued .... 12 Hurricanes engaged a formation of 50 Junkers and their escorting fighters and shot down six of them .... German losses now 394 .... air raid casualties during July were 258 killed, 321 injured ....

11 August: Waves of enemy bombers and fighters launched large-scale attacks during the day on the south east and Channel coasts .... 200 German planes raided Portland and Weymouth .... the enemy lost 65 planes, the British 26 ....

12 August: Further extensive raids by hundreds of enemy aircraft were made on the south coast .... a church and houses were damaged on the Isle of Wight .... casualties very light .... 62 enemy planes brought down, the RAF lost 13 ....

13 August: Hundreds of German planes bombed places from Hampshire to the Thames estuary .... RAF aerodromes were chief targets .... Southampton heavily bombed .... bombs dropped at scattered points in the Midlands and north east Scotland .... 78 German planes brought down, only 13 British fighters were lost ....

14 August: Enemy aircraft activity less pronounced .... barrage balloons attacked at Dover .... a number of parachutes apparently dropped from aircraft found in certain areas of Derbyshire but no parachutists found .... we are all looking out for German spies but no luck yet .... Mum says be very careful .... 31 German planes brought down, 7 British lost ....

15 August: Germany made their greatest attack on Britain so far by sending over 1,000 planes .... RAF aerodromes attacked .... Croydon aerodrome attacked by dive bombers .... 180 enemy planes brought down, 34 British lost but 17 of our pilots were rescued.

16 August: South coast and Isle of Wight attacked, also London suburbs and Tilbury .... RAF aerodromes bombed .... 75 German planes brought down, we lost 22 ....

17 August: German activity slackened but parts of Wales were bombed ....

18 August: Mass raids on south east England and south London with attacks on aerodromes and harbours .... engaged by the RAF and ground defences .... attempts to penetrate London defences broken up .... some casualties at Croydon .... servicemen killed .... 153 enemy machines destroyed, 22 British lost but 10 pilots rescued .... German plane brought down by fire from Home Guards.

I wrote down the aircraft losses each day and started to compile a table. The figures looked like cricket scores and we were winning easily. What we didn't know at the time was that the figures were quite false. Official figures now show that German losses were greatly exaggerated. The reason may have been that two or more of our pilots were each claiming the same victim or maybe the Ministry had boosted the figures to help morale.

German losses on 8 August were 31 planes, not the 60 claimed, on the 13th they lost 45, not 78, on the 15th their losses were 75, not 180, on the 18th they lost 71, not 153. The given British losses were more or less accurate.

On Tuesday 20 August, it was back to school, the Education Committee having decided that this year the summer holiday should be restricted to two full weeks rather than the four weeks we had before the war. We met up with our friends again and everybody agreed that the RAF were beating the

Luftwaffe. When we got home that day Winston Churchill was making a speech. 'Never in the field of human conflict was so much owed by so many to so few.' It made everybody feel good.

My diary had less entries during the next few days as there was a brief respite due to bad weather between 19 and 24 August but the attacks soon resumed and were concentrated on airfields, ports and aircraft factories. Manston was put out of action and Kenley and Biggin Hill suffered serious damage. By the first week in September five stations were not fully operational. The RAF had suffered serious losses, 290 aircraft, many of them on the ground, and about a fifth of our fighter pilots were either killed or wounded. If the Luftwaffe had continued their attacks on RAF bases the south of England would probably have had no fighter cover and the course of the war could have been changed as the loss of fighters was now outstripping the supply of new aircraft. There was also an acute shortage of experienced pilots, Squadrons which should have had an average of twenty six operational pilots only had sixteen. No new squadrons were being formed.

But we knew nothing of this. The Ministry of Information were working overtime censoring the news in order to keep up morale. German air attacks continued, culminating in a huge assault on 15 September of southern England including the Spitfire factory near Southampton. Newspaper headlines screamed out at us the next day that a record 185 German planes had been brought down. In actual fact the correct figure was something like 52 against RAF losses of 26. This was the last of the great daylight air battles over England. It had proved costly to the Luftwaffe and they were now turning their attention to night bombing.

Parades were a way of making people feel good and in mid-August at the height of the Battle of Britain Ilkeston had one of its big parades. Starting at the Town Hall headed by the Stanton Ironworks Band, it proceeded by a circuitous route to St Mary's Church. The long column included police, Home Guards, Fire Brigade, AFS, wardens, St John Ambulance Brigade, First Aid Post personnel, Rescue and Decontamination parties, Boy Scouts and Girl Guides, a total of six hundred uniformed people which slowly wended its way down South Street into White Lion Square, returning by Market Street. Several hundred spectators watched them enter St Mary's where the Bishop of Derby preached a sermon on 'Love Thine Enemies' which many felt to be an inappropriate choice.

The Germans were busy with their propaganda war. Their star performer was William Joyce, a former lieutenant of Oswald Mosley, and nicknamed Lord Haw Haw, whose broadcasts, although widely listened to, were never treated seriously and became something of a joke.

'Jairmany calling, Jairmany calling' the nasal tones announced as Dad picked him up on the Bremen radio station.

'Here he is' said Dad, 'let's see what lies he's got to tell us tonight.' It was usually wildly exaggerated bombing claims of aerodromes or shipping which kept us amused for ten minutes or so.

But our Ministry of Information were not happy at people listening in to him and an advertisement appeared in the papers:

'What do I do .... if I come across German or Italian broadcasts when tuning my wireless? I say to myself: "Now this blighter wants me to listen to him. Am I going to do what he wants?" I remember that German lies over the air are like parachute troops dropping on Britain - they are all part of the plan to get us down - which they won't. I remember nobody can trust a word the Haw-Haws say. So, just to make them waste their time, I switch 'em off or tune 'em out.'

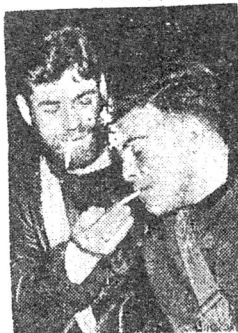

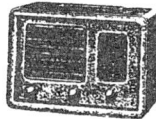

71

CHAPTER EIGHT
RUN FOR THE SHELTER

Night raids started towards the end of August. Our evenings were disrupted by the sound of Wailing Willie, the 'Alert' which signified that enemy aircraft were in the vicinity. My parents had already decided there was only one thing to do: go to the Vernon Street shelter. Each evening we were prepared for the inevitable warning, usually about nine o'clock, when we would put on our coats, scarves and hats, tuck a cushion under our arms - we soon learnt that we needed protection from the hard slatted seats of the shelter - and scurry from the house with dimmed torches up Richmond Avenue and along Cotmanhay Road. The voices of other families making the same journey would pentrate the darkness, their progress marked by faint patches of light.

When Dad was at work Mum, fearful of the blackout with her three children, would enlist the aid of a neighbour to accompany us to the shelter or escort us back after the All Clear. In this way we got to know the obliging Sam Yarrow, Jim Kirk and 'Pop' Elliott much better. When we arrived at the shelter we usually discovered the same people there night after night. The hours passed slowly in the dark and dimly-lit shelter, cigarette smoke trapped in the dank atmosphere. Some families were in conversation, others slept fitfully, others snored. Small children stretched out in siren suits on the hard seats, their heads in the laps of parents, older children vainly trying to stay awake. Sometimes I slept in an upright position, at other times I was lolling on my parents, suddenly to be awakened by a noisy neighbour or the sound of the 'All Clear.'

In the beginning we heard enemy planes passing overhead, to Merseyside, Sheffield and Yorkshire towns and cities. But then, almost a year into the war, the Luftwaffe turned their attention to the Ilkeston district. With 5,000 people employed at Stanton producing 500 lb bombs, inevitably the area became a target.

Stanton Gate foundry was a completely new plant built on 25 acres of farm land. It operated for four years and during that time 873,500 bombs were cast of which 785,000 were delivered to the filling factories. Steel scrap was melted in four cupolas, superheated in two rotary furnaces and charged into four side-blown convertors. The output produced bombs at the rate of a hundred an hour. In one record week 9,350 bombs were produced. There were thirteen machines in the machine shop giving nose-boring and facing to the bombs in an operational time of five minutes per bomb. The output of the machine shop coincided with that of the foundry. Work was on a two shift system and many women were employed in the machine shop. It was arduous work in the unheated buildings, especially in winter. Later in the war Italian prisoners of war were drafted in. Air raid shelters including some gas-proof ones were also produced at Stanton which had its own fire brigade.

At 2 am on 28 August seven high explosive bombs were dropped in Rushy Lane Sandiacre and at Dale Road in Stanton-by-Dale. Four of them were delayed action but all exploded before daylight. The only damage however was to roads and there were no casualties.

That night the bombers were back, dropping incendiaries in the same area followed by two high explosive bombs, one near Twelve Houses at the entrance to the concrete pipe seasoning field which exploded on impact causing little damage, and one near the junction of Stanton Lane and Lowes Lane, a delayed action bomb which exploded about 3 am, fracturing gas and water mains and closing the road for a few days. About the same time, a high explosive bomb was dropped in Shipley Woods without damage or casualties.

In the early hours of the morning of 30 August a German plane dropped a couple of incendiaries at the rear of the Sevenoaks Inn, again without damage or casualties.

However, the worst was to come. At eleven o'clock that night, high explosive bombs and incendiaries were dropped on the Gallows Inn area of Ilkeston. Residents, many of whom were in their gardens or blacked-out streets (contrary to ARP advice needless to say) were soon diving for cover when bombs and incendiaries began raining down.

One family that did so was the Collisters living at The Triangle. Denis and Jessie Collister and their eight year old daughter Pat were standing in their garden by their home-made air raid shelter which was a deep trench topped by railway sleepers with steps cut out of the earth leading to an entrance door. They watched incendiaries falling towards the canal, the water providing a perfect landmark for the bombers to follow. Although the blackout was strictly enforced the glint of the water in the moonlight could not be suppressed, in fact the whole area from Trent Junction where the Trent and Derwent rivers met and a system of railway lines to Nottingham, Derby and Sheffield formed a trident and could easily be seen from the air.

It was about ten minutes past eleven when the Collisters heard the first bomb with its stabilising fins whistling towards them. They dived into the shelter like rabbits into a burrow. They had just passed through the door of the shelter when the thud came from a matter of yards away. Mercifully it did not explode but the shelter caved in engulfing them with damp earth and railway sleepers, one of which struck Pat on the head and pitching her parents to the floor.

Today Pat recalls that it seemed an eternity in the pitch darkness, blacker than anything she ever knew before or since, dazed and wet from the earth, waiting for the explosion which never came.

Her father produced matches from his pocket (one advantage of being a smoker) and began searching amongst the debris for the candles he kept in the trench. On finding and lighting a candle, he stumbled across his garden spade, thoughtfully kept in the shelter, and proceeded to dig his way out, eventually emerging with his family, all caked in mud.

The garden was a battlefield; the house was still standing although many windows were broken. Shaken and bruised and covered in mud they decided to leave the area fearing the bomb would explode. With Pat still in her night attire and an over-large coat of her mother's, they made their way along the road lit by flames from incendiaries to the nearby Charnos factory where Denis was Chief Mechanic, the air heavy with the acrid smell of burning. They took refuge in the firm's silk waste store in the basement where the resident cats had also taken cover.

When the 'All Clear' sounded some time later they made their way back towards their house only to be stopped by wardens and police who told them the whole area was out of bounds due to the unexploded bombs. The only thing they could do was to get in their car which was parked in a wooden shed by the canal and drive to a farm owned by friends at West Hallam where they were given shelter until they could return to their own home.

Several other high explosive bombs fell that night, one at the junction of Glebe Crescent and Greenwood Avenue causing damage to water and gas mains; one on Brook Street resulting in a crater in the road; one at the rear of Mace's furniture shop on Nottingham Road; one at Larklands Avenue which went through the roof and rear bedroom of number 36 burying itself under the ground floor; and one on the Corporation tip at Gallows Inn.

Remarkably, there were no serious casualties as the only bomb which exploded was the one on the tip which caused extensive damage to the Gallows Inn sewage pumping station and numerous houses on Corporation Road.

At the other end of the town we heard the distant action from the relative safety of the Vernon Street public shelter.

'Hallam Fields is getting it' agreed several shadowy figures in the densely packed shelter, lit only by two or three bulbs. 'It might be us next.'

By midnight the bombing seemed to have stopped although we could still hear the droning of enemy planes and sporadic gunfire. We were beginning to think the worst was over and I was beginning to drop off to sleep leaning against my mother's shoulder when there were sudden bangs and explosions.

'They're right overhead' called out a warden standing near the entrance of the shelter. 'They're dropping bombs. Stay put everybody.'

I could feel my mother shaking. 'Oh dear, what's going to happen to us.' She was a great worrier, even when there nothing to worry about. But this was different; we had never had bombs exploding around us before. My father was consoling her and a neighbour opposite assured her 'You'll be all right duck.'

Anti-aircraft guns were pounding away including a large naval gun situated at Shipley Common nicknamed 'Big Bertha.'

'They'll shoot the b's' down' the neighbour assured my mother confidently. There was a lull with the sound of aircraft engines receding. 'They've gone' said a voice. A few minutes later however they were back. More 'Oh dears' from Mum.

We heard the guns hammering away, then more explosions. 'Right overhead' said the warden. 'Stay put.'

That's all we could do, stay put. Our fate was in the hands of the bombers. Everybody was awake and attentive, quite unlike other nights in the shelter when people dozed off. People were apprehensive, some like my mother very worried, but nobody panicked.

After four o'clock the noises died down and we emerged from the shelter just as dawn was breaking. We were told that h.e. bombs had exploded at Shipley and Skevington's Lane, quite close to home, but there was no damage or casualties.

Ilkeston's worst night of bombing however came a few days later in the early hours of 5 September. The alert had sounded and people were packed into shelters, public and private, while others used a ground floor room or cellar, whichever was deemed to be the safest.

Mark Hallam and his family were using the spacious shelter he had built in his garden at Little Hallam Lane together with three other families. Eight year old Jeff Hallam remembers the All Clear sounding and returning to the house and to bed at about 4 am. He had just dropped off to sleep when he awoke to a blinding flash and the sound of explosions. It was mayhem as the families raced back into the shelter, the children puzzled as they thought the All Clear a few minutes earlier meant the raiders had gone away.

Now it sounded as if there was a full scale war outside, a cacophony of sound of planes, guns and bombs. Eventually things quietened down and they emerged to find the windows of their house blown out and the bedroom ceiling of Jeff's sister blown down.

Morning revealed that Jerry had dropped a stick of high explosive bombs, the first of which had exploded within a hundred yards of the Hallam's house. Jeff remembers seeing three houses totally destroyed and many more badly damaged.

'The houses were hanging in tatters' was how he described it, an apt description. Houses fifty yards away from one bomb had their bedroom windows and whole frames sucked into their gardens. As well as police and wardens cordoning off the area and First Aid Parties and Demolition Squads on hand, crowds of sightseers were appearing, making things more difficult for those dealing with the situation.

Jeff met up with his cousin Gordon who was excitedly holding up a souvenir, a large piece of the actual bomb casing. Small boys and not-so-small boys were searching the area for pieces of shrapnel and other souvenirs. This led to trading and swopping, especially at school where boys were turning up with all sorts of objects. Cyril Charlton remembers picking up shrapnel in Cotmanhay Road. Items were being labelled and collections formed by those who at one time would have been collecting cigarette cards (now discontinued by the tobacco companies because of the war) and various pieces were on offer at school. I was offered and bought for twopence a piece of shrapnel, an astute buy I thought. However when I proudly showed it to some classmates they all laughed and said it was just a lump of lead. An early lesson in buying collectables: never take at face value what somebody tells you and only buy with knowledge. My twopence would have been better spent on a quarter of liquorice allsorts.

Mercifully noboby was killed in the raid on Ilkeston in spite of the serious damage to houses. 3 Inglefield Road, unoccupied at the time, was destroyed (later rebuilt) and its neighbour number 5 seriously damaged. The row of houses 363 to 373 (odds) Nottingham Road were so badly damaged it was decided to demolish them. Luckily they were empty at the time due to the unexploded bombs in the area from the previous week's raid. However many families had to leave their homes and temporary accommodation was found at South Street Schools and private houses in the town secured by the Billeting Officer. At one stage no food was available for the displaced families so the Town Clerk produced some by breaking into a warehouse for bread and a dairy for milk. A rare example of a Town Clerk breaking and entering!

Demolition work and repairs were carried out speedily following a letter from the Ministry of Health the following week which urged authorities 'to proceed with carrying out first aid repairs to property with the utmost speed to maintain public morale.' You could see what they meant. Looking at a row of houses with roofs and walls missing, some with items of furniture balanced precariously from bedrooms, did not improve spirits.

Building materials from the demolished houses were purchased by the Corporation for £10 to £15 per house, and estimates for repairs to damaged houses quickly obtained, varying from £15 for number 4 Inglefield Road to £160 for number 5. It is interesting to note that the values placed on the houses at that time were in the region of £350 to £435 for the Inglefield Road properties. Repairs were also needed to the Gallows Inn pumping station caused by two high explosive bombs; the cost of this was £152.

By the end of October a report from the Borough Surveyor showed that 'first aid' repairs (as opposed to permanent repairs) had been carried out on 484 houses: admittedly many of these would be of a minor nature such as broken windows. By 30 November repairs had been made to 622 houses.

Theories have been put forward that some of the bombs dropped in the Gallows Inn area of Ilkeston were not intended for Stanton at all but for the Rolls Royce aero-engine plant at Derby. This could well be.

On the last Sunday afternoon in September a single German raider, said to be a Heinkel 111, attempted to bomb Stanton. It was a pleasant day and Cyril Charlton and his father were in their backyard when they first saw the plane flying south down the Erewash valley.

'That's a German bomber!' exclaimed Cyril excitedly.

'Niver' said his father.

They watched it fly towards Stanton Ironworks where molten iron was being run into the pig beds, a job that was done during the day rather than night when it would have illuminated the area. Suddenly Cyril saw the bomb doors open and three bombs flash to the ground. The upshot was that one bomb exploded causing damage to the canal bank. Stanton escaped although some debris was blown on to the main railway line.

The only other war damage to Ilkeston properties occurred on the night of 26 November when a barrage balloon which had broken away from its moorings drifted towards the buildings at the bottom of Bath Street and caught overhead wires. Damage was caused to roofs and windows as the monster bounced into Lord Haddon Road, then Pelham Street where it was pursued by ARP workers who never really stood a chance of securing it. It proceeded into Tutin Street, did a rhumba in the gasworks and then made off towards Cossall.

Much has been written about the blitz. The first bombs fell on central London on 24 August 1940 followed by attacks on Liverpool on the nights of 28, 29, 30 and 31 August, the same nights that Ilkeston and district was bombed.

On the afternoon of Saturday 7 September the Luftwaffe launched a mass attack on the East End of London. Enormous damage was done to the docks, thousands of homes were destroyed, 430 civilians were killed and 1,600 seriously injured. The bombers returned the following evening when another four hundred were killed. Firemen and ARP wardens were overwhelmed, the docks were an inferno.

Night after night the bombers returned. On 9 September 370 were killed. The following night they were back gutting St Katherine's Dock in what was believed to be the worst fire England had ever known. All the warehouses containing vital materials were destroyed. The homes left standing had no gas, electricity or water.

Newspapers and radio reports informed us that 'morale was good' and the

East Enders remained cheerful, The Times declaring that people 'were not going to flinch until mastery (over the enemy) was won'. Such reports put out by the Ministry of Information were often accompanied by pictures of smiling Cockneys with thumbs up against a background of rubble.

However, secret Mass Observation reports taken at the time said that morale was low and one raid had provoked panic. People were packed in insanitary air raid shelters and tube stations, some without toilets. Fifteen miles of platforms and tunnels housed 170,000 on one night. Bombs seriously damaged the stations at Trafalgar Square where seven were killed, Balham (64 killed) and Bank (111 killed).

Londoners felt very much at the mercy of the German bombers and wanted to know what was being done about it. They wanted to hear gunfire but it wasn't there. The reason was apparently that the enemy was being tackled by our night fighters, but the public could see little sign of this as the bombers were overhead for hours on end, wave after wave queueing up to drop their deadly cargo.

Fearing anti-war demonstrations the Government decided to bring in the guns and although not very effective (it was said that it took on average 10,000 shells to be fired before an enemy plane was brought down) it did make people feel better when the guns opened up. In Ilkeston I remember people shouting 'give it to 'em' as the naval type gun opened up with great ferocity on Shipley Common as planes passing overhead for Merseyside. Young Cyril Charlton living on Vernon Street remembers it as a three inch gun set in concrete and the first time it was fired resulted in the panes of a nearby greenhouse dropping out. Cyril also recalls a night when a German bomber, picked out by searchlights, was shot down by the gun crew resulting in the landlord of the Rutland Cottage Inn (or 'Brealeys' as it was known after a former owner) pulling free pints all round.

Many Londoners fled the capital, travelling into the provinces with a few belongings by bus, train and car. Many who had been evacuated a year earlier were leaving again. This caused problems in many towns and villages round London when hundreds, sometimes thousands, would descend demanding accommodation.

The attacks on London continued and the Luftwaffe also started to turn its attention to the provinces. Birmingham was bombed and 170 people killed but worse was to come. On the night of 14 November 1940 Coventry was attacked with great intensity, devastating the whole of the city centre: even from Ilkeston the red glow of the blazing city could be seen, in fact some Ilkeston firemen joined those from other towns in helping to deal with the conflagration.

Four hundred German bombers had appeared over Coventry just after seven o'clock in the evening, first dropping flares to light up the city, then 30,000 incendiaries (some with explosive charges) followed by 500 tons of landmines and high explosive bombs. Over 550 civilians and 26 firemen lost their lives, 865 civilians and 200 firemen were seriously injured. These were enormous losses for a relatively small city (population in 1938 was 213,000) and a new word was coined, to 'Coventrate', meaning complete destruction of a city. Later in the war, Dresden and Hiroshima were to share similar fates.

One of the most serious problems in the blitz was fire caused by incendiaries and the authorities were very slow off the mark in taking measures. Although fire parties were well organised in some areas, in others they were thin on the ground, Some householders had buckets of water and sand at the ready (a few even had stirrup pumps bought at their own expense), others did not.

The most serious problem was unoccupied buildings including commercial and industrial premises at nightime. It wasn't until January 1941 that the Government finally took action to make fire watching compulsory - months after the commencement of the blitz. Men between sixteen and sixty were compelled to do a maximum of 48 hours a month. Many people tried to dodge this, pleading they were one of the exceptions. The courts began to get tough with the dodgers and several appeared before the magistrates and fined, usually between ten shillings and £2.

In January Captain Kilford of the Ilkeston Fire Brigade reported there were seventy fire watching parties in the town and stirrup pumps had been issued to parties of three or more. Commercial areas were well covered but some residential areas were not being watched. The manager of Montagu Burton had taken the lead in Bath Street and had 32 men under his control, each of whom had been issued with a torch.

About fifty sand dumps had appeared in various parts of the town for use in tackling incendiaries and householders were permitted to collect half a hundred weight each, about two buckets full, but I heard people complaining they didn't have two buckets!

The Government was constantly issuing advice including not to sit round your coal fire (everybody in Ilkeston had a coal fire) during an air raid as casualties had been caused by fires being blown out of the grate by bomb blast.

At this time the regular Ilkeston Fire Brigade numbered 24 men including three officers. Its equipment included a turbine capable of pumping 450 gallons a minute, a 60 foot escape, extinguishers and 2500 feet of hose on the engine. The first aid engine was equipped with a 40 gallon tank which would last for ten minutes; most fires were put out by this engine.

The station was manned at night as was the AFS (Auxiliary Fire Service) headquarters in Stanton Road. There were also three auxiliary stations in the town. Counting AFS men, there was a total of 37 full time officers and men and 130 part timers. Six cars and four lorries were also connected direct with the control room and plans were in hand to install a phone at the top of the highest building in the town, connected direct to the AFS station.

During the raids on Ilkeston of August and September 1940, 250 to 300 incendiaries had been dropped and dealt with in 15 minutes, it was claimed. There were three 3,500 gallon water tanks in the town, at the Rutland Hotel, Kings Picture House and one near the top of Derby Road.

CHAPTER NINE
CHRISTMAS SHOPPING IN THE DARK

Life in Ilkeston during the autumn of 1940 was going on under wartime conditions. In October we had a half term school holiday of eight days but were disappointed to find that the annual fair had been cancelled. The four picture houses were doing good business and I went to see Will Hay in 'Oh Mr Porter' at the Scala which I thought very funny, as well as the horrors of Dracula and Frankenstein which the Scala liked to put on. I also watched war and cowboy films at the others. Of course we grumbled when the cheapest seats went up from 6d to 8d (because of tax we were told) although I could still get in at half price.

People at the top were beginning to recognise that entertainment for youngsters was very limited in Ilkeston - 'We're browned off' was a favourite expression - and we heard that a group of people led by our form teacher, Mr A.D. Nash, were trying to form a youth club by starting a 'Shilling Fund.' As a result the Pines Youth Club was later opened in Stanton Road.

Adults were flocking to dance halls, especially the New Co-op Hall in the Market Place which had opened in the Spring. Built to seat 900 people for public meetings, it was also a popular venue for big dances and there was now less need for people to travel to Nottingham or Derby. The New Co-op started their autumn programme with a 'Grand Flash Dance.' Their advert asked 'Can you flash?' and promised a 'Blitzkrieg of prizes', presumably to the best flashers although I hadn't a clue what flashing was. Dancing was between six and nine in the evening or 'safety hours' which many dance halls operated. Admission was one shilling and threepence.

Christmas dancing at the New Co-op Hall included a 'Gigantic Xmas Carnival Dance' and a 'Grand Mistletoe Dance' with the promise of hats, streamers, balloons and novelties, as well as a 'Grand Christmas Children's Carnival Dance' with Nan Smedley's dancers putting on a show and gifts for everyone from Santa Claus. Every event seemed to be prefixed by the word 'Grand.'

Many churches were holding Christmas bazaars (I expect these were Grand, too) and of course the Spitfire Exhibition of model aircraft and engineering was attracting crowds. Volunteers were making up parcels for the Mayor's Comforts Fund. There were now 2,000 local men and women serving in the Forces and each one received a parcel to the value of five shillings. This was quite a formidable task as the organisers discovered. There was no problem about getting khaki handkerchiefs and socks - many volunteers were knitting like fury - one lady had knitted 83 pairs of socks in a fortnight on her machine - but there were big problems in obtaining sweets which had become very scarce as I had discovered - all my favourites had disappeared from the shops. Even when they had sufficient goodies to put in the parcels, there was still a great deal of work in making them up, a task mainly undertaken by the WVS. The Mayor probably had the best solution: it would be easier in future to send a five shilling postal order. The money was raised by house to house collections and donations. Many firms sent gifts of money to their employees serving in the Forces. Ilkeston Co-op and the firm of A.E. Booth each sent out a generous gift of £1.

The shops were expecting extra business in spite of wartime shortages. Mum and Dad looked in at Greaves the furnishers whose slogan was 'Christmas will come despite Hitler.' From their large stock of furniture - '£40,000 worth free of tax' according to their notice - my parents chose a small carpet. Gifts were also 'free of tax' at Woods in Bath Street where I saw gift sets, perfumes, cameras and hot water bottles, and if you wanted to make merry G.F. Thompson was offering Scotch and Irish whiskies, gin, rum, brandy, ports, sherries and British wines. On the other hand Foster Brothers Clothing Company took an advert in the paper to extend Christmas greetings to their customers as 'we have no need to advertise this week as we are already almost embarrassingly busy.'

As I went round the shops after school to buy Christmas presents for the rest of the family I was struck by the gloom, the badly-lit shops with blackout curtains, people wandering about with dimmed torches peering at impoverished stocks on the counters, customers enquiring about items to be told 'Sorry, sold out' or 'We've not had any this year.' Even Woolworth's, usually a treat to visit with its long counters of toys, gifts, sweets and Christmas decorations, looked drab. The sweet counter was almost bare, no chocolate at all, so I had to settle for mint imperials for Margaret and

Children's Corner

CHRISTMAS, 1940

By Garnet Langton, aged 12

Although Christmas 1940 was a wartime Christmas, it was both happy and exciting. I must admit that I was excited when I came down on Christmas morning to find out what presents were waiting for me. The one I liked the best was an atlas which was illustrated with many maps in full colour and explained by a gazeteer. I had other books, including "I was Graf Spee's Prisoner," "Captain Albert Ball, V.C., D.S.O.," "The First Six Months of the War," and the "Complete Self-Educator." I also had a number of Meccano parts and several bars of chocolate. A jigsaw was also added to my presents.

I was kept busy Christmas day and many following days reading, building models with my Meccano, and eating Christmas fare at intervals.

Now I will turn to the war point of view. We could not have received our Christmas presents and other good things had it not been for the Royal Navy. The naval men are working night and day for our sake, and we cannot repay them. But we can give them praise, and every time we receive a gift we must thank the sailors.

The 1940 Christmas did differ slightly from a peacetime Christmas. In most cases people did not receive so many presents for the simple reason that the prices had increased, and goods suitable for presents were scarce compared with a peace-time Christmas. But most of us enjoyed a happy Christmas, and everyone was glad it was free from enemy air activity.

82

Trevor's Christmas presents and handkerchiefs for Mum and Dad - I managed to get some white ones for Dad, not the horrible khaki ones. The brightly lit shops and enticing displays of two years ago were just a faded memory.

I was attracted to a competition the Advertiser were running to write a letter 'How I spent Christmas Day.' After writing my piece I handed it in at the Advertiser office on Heanor Road and eagerly awaited the result. As the days and weeks went by without any news I gave up hope until one Friday in March Dad suddenly called out 'You've won!' There it was, in print, with an invitation to call at the newspaper office to collect the prize. When I arrived I met the Editor herself, Miss Shakespeare, who offered me a choice from a whole range of books. After much deliberation I chose R.D. Blackmore's Lorna Doone which I still possess.

In October 1940 huge piles of bricks began appearing in the streets of Ilkeston. They were often delivered hot from the kilns watched by local inhabitants who sometimes joined in the delivery process. In Kingsway and Queens Avenue Jeff Hallam remembers stacking the hot gritty bricks. This may have been a bit of light relief to the children but to the elderly, infirm and mothers with prams the piles of bricks were a menace and in the blackout they caused many accidents.

Workmen eventually appeared and started erecting communal surface shelters. The ARP and Civil Defence Committee of the Town Council had placed an initial order of a million bricks, but as these were used more lorry loads appeared as well as piles of sand and bags of cement: some streets began to look like building sites. In all four or five hundred brick shelters were built including about a hundred and fifty in the central area of the town. Most were in side streets, some on waste land. The smallest shelters were for half a dozen people, the largest 48. There were restrictions as to who could use them and these families were notified by the Town Hall. Qualifying families were those whose incomes did not exceed £250 a year which probably covered a fair proportion of the population.

However they were unpopular, and few families used them. With their flat concrete roofs, they looked more like a garages than shelters. Inside they had long slatted benches like the underground shelters. A few had lights and lavatories but people did not really feel safe in them as they did underground. The two shelters I used - Vernon Street and Hallcroft School - were both sunk into the ground with earth on the top.

The shelters were invariably damp and although experiments were made with waterproofing and ventilation, the problem was not solved. Shelters were the targets for vandals and several people came before the courts for causing damage. They were often used as toilets, especially those near pubs, and other uses included 'immoral purposes' according to a member of the Town Council.

The best underground shelters of course were in London, the Underground itself, which was used nightly by thousands of people during the blitz. Caves were used in some parts of the country - the Peak District for instance - but I never heard of anyone using the hermit's cave at Dale Abbey.

The Anderson shelters were six curved steel plates bolted together at the top to form an arch with flat steel plates fixed at either end. One end had an opening for entrance, the other end could be unbolted as an emergency exit. It stood in a trench about four feet deep and was covered with earth; some grew plants or vegetables on top. They were six feet six inches in length and were meant for six people. The first consignment of 250 started to arrive in Ilkeston in January 1941, part of the one thousand allocated to the town. I believe the rest didn't arrive until months later, far too late to be of any use as bombing had virtually finished.

A few families had Morrison shelters, named after Herbert Morrison, Minister of Home Security. They were for indoor use, about two feet nine inches high, wire mesh sides with a steel plate on top which could be used as a table during the day.

Public shelters had been provided after a great amount of pressure. After the raids on Ilkeston at the end of August and beginning of September - the only serious raids made on the town as it transpired - there was concern about the inadequacy of public shelter accommodation. A public meeting in Wilmot Street Schools in July had demanded more shelters, Anderson and communal, 'in no uncertain manner' according to the Advertiser. A total of 2,146 signatures had been obtained for a petition and this was being presented to the Town Council.

As we watched the shelters being built, the Town Council were planning their next project, Rest Centres. The idea was to provide temporary accommodation for homeless people in the event of more raids. The bombings in August and September had shown how little the town was prepared when only South Street Schools had been available with no provision at all to feed people. Other schools in the town would therefore be used for any future emergency. The blitz was still continuing, after all we heard enemy planes overhead on their way to Merseyside most nights as we huddled in the shelters.

The first Rest Centre opened at Cavendish School at the end of February. There was a Grand Opening of course - every opportunity was made during the war to rally the people and turn it into a civic occasion - when Alderman Sudbury said that 'under this platform we have hundreds of pounds worth of food and everything necessary to provide meals' including 729 lb of tinned meat, 16 tea urns, 738 lb of sugar, 91 lb of jam and other foods. The Centre was equipped with 34 wash basins, 230 mattresses, 667 blankets, 400 pillows, 414 towels - a formidable amount during this wartime period. Bennerley Rest Centre opened in the infants' school a couple of weeks later followed by Centres at Gladstone, Granby, Kensington, Chaucer and County Secondary School.

Now we had a Rest Centre on our doorstep; somewhere to go if we were bombed out. I noticed that there were plenty of comings and goings when it opened, mostly women in green uniforms. They were the Women's Voluntary Service under their superintendent, Mrs Alfred Booth, and they appeared to be running the Centre.

The WVS had been formed in 1938 by Lady Reading and at the outbreak of war had 336,000 members. By 1941 it had grown to a million. They were nearly all unpaid (I think they even bought their own uniforms) and whenever help was needed they were usually there: at the evacuation of children, looking after troops returning from Dunkirk, running mobile canteens, providing food and drink during the blitz, organising emergency clothing and transport, giving first aid, collecting salvage, and now they were looking after the new Rest Centres. Also helping were local teachers.

Another use to which schools were put was adult education. In the winter of 1940-41 classes organised by the Ilkeston Evening Institute were being held at various schools in the town, for instance at the County Secondary School there were classes in engineering, foundry work, building trades, plumbing and other commercial subjects while at Cavendish there were junior technical engineering courses.

At Cotmanhay women neighbours were attending Bennerley Schools in the evenings for cookery, needlework and dressmaking. These proved very popular as women were discovering new ways of adding variety to their meals and also 'keeping up appearances' with the shortage of clothing. The nation was looking shabbier as restrictions were put on clothing manufacture for the home market as many firms had turned over to war production such as service uniforms and parachutes. The days when everybody liked to dress up on Sunday had gone, in fact many people were now working on Sunday and you could see people in overalls on the Sabbath almost as much as on a weekday.

Inevitably we had to have clothes rationing and this came into force on 1 June 1941 and lasted until 1949. Each adult was allowed 66 coupons a year, later reduced to 60 over 15 months in 1942. This led to some serious decisions having to be made.

'Let's see, fourteen coupons for a coat, five for a pair of shoes and I want two pairs of stockings, that's another four coupons. Altogether that's 23. I shall have to be careful. Lucky I've got some wool to knit myself a dress, otherwise that would have been another eleven ....'

Mum was doing her arithmetic like everybody else. Clothes rationing was not too bad for those who already had large wardrobes but to the poor it came as a blow. There was much patching and darning ('Make do and Mend' was the expression), people borrowed, swapped and passed down their clothes. When clothes began to look tired they were sometimes dyed, occasionally remodelled. Women began wearing slacks - seldom seen before the war - saving the need for stockings. Some women who went without stockings in summer used leg make-up, sometimes pencilling a line down the back of their legs to represent a seam. Shoes were made to last longer by adding stick-on soles.

Then we had the Utility scheme, under which clothes were produced with simple designs, cutting out the trimmings in order to save cloth. They had a special label, were good value and had to be of a certain standard, usually hard wearing, but they took a little getting used to at first. I remember Dad buying a new suit. The first time he put it on, I looked at him with some astonishment.

'But your trousers have got no turn-ups.'

'Turn-ups have been abolished' he told me. 'It's the new Utility scheme. Don't you like it?'

I didn't like it, I'd never seen trousers before without turn-ups; I thought they were ridiculous.

'Well, when we buy you a suit, yours will have no turn-ups either' he told me.

He was right but nobody liked it and there was a public outcry. This led Hugh Dalton, President of the Board of Trade, to remark 'Some must lose lives and limbs, others only their turn-ups.' I was glad I had just gone into long trousers because shortly afterwards clothing firms were only making short trousers for younger boys up to about eleven or twelve.

In the Spring of 1941 I noticed a new shop had opened in the Ritz buildings on South Street which was unusual as you hardly ever saw new shops opening. It was called the Citizen's Advice Bureau. There was nothing for sale, just posters and notices in the window about helping people with their problems and giving the opening hours: Tuesday mornings, Thursday evenings and Saturday afternoons. It was an unusual place but I was told they were opening in all large towns. As I didn't have any particular problems except not enough pocket money I didn't think they could help me.

87

CHAPTER TEN
IT'S ONE OF OURS

Plane spotting was the schoolboy craze of the early forties. Newspapers, magazines, pamphlets, booklets and books were full of pictures and illustrations of aircraft, friend and foe. Some helpfully gave 'points of recognition,' and we became familiar with radial motors, tapered wings, swept back leading edges, dihedrals, angular single fins, retracting undercarriages and all kinds of other aircraft jargon. A large chart was pinned to my bedroom wall with illustrations and silhouettes of the types of aircraft we were most likely to see. Every time a plane went over, my eyes turned skywards.

Suddenly the hobby was given a boost at the beginning of 1941 when a new publication called the Aeroplane Spotter appeared. Pictures and silhouettes of the latest aircraft were depicted in detail so that I could register the shapes of wings, fuselages and tails of bombers, fighters and reconnaisance planes which were appearinmg in our skies. As well as the illustrations there were also articles written in technical jargon, thus the Fairey Swordfish was identified as a one and a half bay braced biplane of unequal span and cord with a marked dihedral on top main planes but no dihedral on bottom planes, a radial motor with short cord cowling, big rounded single fin and rudder and fixed tripod undercarriage. When I showed this to Mum and Dad and they saw the paper's sub-title ('For The Alert') they were most impressed and agreed it was well worth the threepence a week which had been added to the newsagent's bill.

Thursdays - the day the Spotter arrived - was a red letter day. I was up early awaiting the appearance of the paper boy with a laden bag attached to his cycle, who stopped occasionally to read the latest exploits of Big Eggo in the Beano or Desperate Dan in the Dandy while I watched him impatiently behind curtains. To my annoyance he often thumbed the pages of my Spotter, even though it was encased in Dad's Daily Herald, before pushing it through the letter box where I was waiting to seize on it.

Of course this coincided with breakfast to which my mother gave a higher priority than the Spotter ('Drink your tea and eat your egg before it goes cold') but most of my attention was for the latest planes and their performances, being careful of course to avoid fat, grease or tea stains from spoiling the cherished paper which I preserved in a neat pile in my bedroom for constant reference.

There were articles on latest developments in aircraft production and weekly notes for spotters which showed distinguishing features between similar types of plane, especially between British and German planes which was deemed to be most important, after all we didn't want to be caught waving to what we thought was a Hurricane only for it to turn out to be a Messerschmitt 109 diving towards us with machine guns blazing. Accurate spotting was not easy; at the time there were about four hundred types of aircraft flying in Europe.

The Aeroplane Spotter turned out to be a very popular paper. Although there was a wartime ban on starting new magazines and newspapers, this was waived in the case of the Spotter as it was helping the war effort in identifying planes, especially amongst service and civil air defences. One condition was imposed, that it should carry no advertising. Within two years it was selling a hundred thousand copies an issue and could have sold more if sufficient newsprint had been available.

My regular order started with the first issue, 2 January 1941, and was carefully noted in my diary. Gradually the pile of Spotters in my bedroom grew but then came a calamity. One Thursday I proudly took the latest issue to school. At the end of the day I raised my desk lid to discover it was missing. Nobody had asked to borrow it so had it been stolen?

I was distraught. I knew that the little paper was in demand, but never realised that people would steal it. I was chasing around seeking clues, asking my friends, but eventually drew a blank. There were plenty of sympathetic noises but no one could help. I was down in the dumps as I faced the weekend without my beloved Spotter. A long miserable weekend followed by Monday morning back at school. But as I raised the lid of my desk, the clouds lifted too and the sun was shining again: there lay a replacement Spotter, crisp and new. I never did discover who put it there but I almost began to believe in fairies again.

Making models of planes from kits was a popular pastime with several classmates but it made no appeal to me. Instead I began drawing planes, first in a sketchbook in pencil, then more ambitiously on large sheets of paper. Unused rolls of wallpaper were just the job: using the unpatterned side I created large pictures of aircraft in water colour from an old paintbox.

After a time I became more ambitious and set off for Walkers, high class stationers and suppliers of art materials, where I purchased indian ink, poster paints and large sheets of cardboard (the latter must have been some of their old pre-war stock) to produce more permanent pictures, some of individual aircraft, others with German planes being shot down by the British, others in the form of a chart with illustrations and details of several aircraft ('The Handley Page Hampden has a maximum speed of 265 m.p.h. and can climb at 980 feet a minute').

Before long the Langton household had drawings of planes decorating the walls, at first welcomed by my parents ('isn't that good, looks real with its guns firing') but when my artistic efforts began to dominate the kitchen and 'front room', completely obscuring the Boyhood of Raleigh and a couple of moonlight scenes featuring romantic couples given to my parents as wedding presents in 1920, they began to throw out hints that we might have more than enough Spitfires, Blenheims and Avro Ansons on view at one time and the numbers should be restricted or even cut back.

Meanwhile my output of aircraft drawings and paintings continued; the smaller ones were kept in a folder, the larger ones behind the wardrobe in my bedroom. Some I gave away including one or two to my grandmother who thought they were 'clever' and a few to rather surprised friends who perhaps thought there might be some ulterior motive, but an attempt to give one to my brother as a birthday present backfired ('I want a proper present, not one of your drawings').

Word got around that I could draw and paint aeroplanes and one day in April 1941 I was told that a couple of local ladies whom I did not know wanted to see me: would I call at their house in Bridge Street, a couple of streets away.

I went to the address which had a notice WARDEN'S POST Q2 above the door with buckets of sand outside. I was ushered in to see the two ladies - Miss Wheatley and Miss Syson I believe - into a room that had charts on the walls, tin hats hanging from pegs, a quantity of arm bands, first aid kits, stirrup pumps and a large table on which were ARP leaflets, a large register apparently to record 'incidents', notebooks and papers. There were also National Savings posters adorning the walls and leaflets urging us to buy savings certificates and stamps.

'Ah, we heard you were good at art and wondered if you could do some National Savings posters for our group?' The local group which they ran covered the area from Bridge Street to Nelson Street including both sides of Cotmanhay Road and the streets leading off.

'It's War Weapons Week at the end of the month and our group has set a target of £400 and we want someone to do posters for us to display in shops and houses in Cotmanhay. Will you do it?'

At twelve years of age having my work acknowledged in a Warden's Post in which I had never set foot before by two charming ladies in the presence of a warden in a tin hat and being requested to do something of national importance, I could hardly refuse. They produced sheets of cardboard, cartridge paper, pots of poster paint and brushes and proceeded to give me instructions.

I was ten feet tall as I hurried home armed with the materials, certain that everybody was looking at me. How many of them realised the role I was about to play in the war effort? I wanted to call out and tell them: 'Hey, I'm doing the posters for War Weapons Week, work of national importance.' This was my Big Effort. I might not had much success with collecting newspapers for salvage - Dad used ours to light the fire - but this was something really vital.

My parent's eyes lit up as I told them of my assignment. 'That's a feather in your cap' said Mum. 'Make sure your teachers know' said Dad.

Preparations started immediately. It had to be done on the kitchen table of course. The table with its chenille cloth and dangling tassels was used for about everything, not just meals. It was for homework, playing cards (whist in the evenings when Dad was on the day shift, patience when I played on my own), Mum's dressmaking and machining, filling out the football coupon every Wednesday, by Dad for writing out his betting slips, by Trevor with his train layout, by me for building Meccano and a dozen other jobs. The underneath had also been used as a dungeon, a cave and a wigwam. Now the table was a drawing board.

When it was cleared and a newspaper placed to protect the chenille cloth ('we don't want it spoilt with paint'), a piece of card was roughed out in pencil with the layout incorporating silhouettes of tanks, guns and planes and in bold lettering WAR WEAPONS WEEK, 25 APRIL - 3 MAY 1941. Also in prominent letters I inscribed THANK THE RANKS WITH TANKS, the winning slogan in a local competition. I then added the local organiser's name and address who would arrange for someone to call each week with savings stamps. For good measure I embellished the poster with a couple of Union Jacks.

There were three or four posters to do which took several sessions. One was a barometer for a main road shop to indicate the amount raised during the week. This was marked off in £s up to £500 with the word TARGET placed at the £400 mark; the arrangement was that the organiser would mark the amount raised in red ink on a daily basis.

This was part of the Government's National Savings campaign, given huge publicity during the war, to persude us to save: quite the opposite of today's consumer society when we are urged to spend, spend, spend. I remember a cartoon character called Squander Bug, a horrible looking insect tattooed with swastikas, imploring people to spend money, with a rhyming ditty urging us to ignore him and put our cash into National Savings. Unnecesssary spending was unpatriotic and you were helping the enemy by indulging youself.

It is true that there were fewer goods to spend money on: food was rationed and other shops were half empty as goods produced for the home market were severely cut back. On the other hand there was plenty of money around. Apart from service men and women and their families who were badly paid, nearly everyone, particularly the working class, found themselves much better off than before the war as they were now working full time with plenty of overtime available, in marked contrast to pre-war conditions.

Men were taking home £4 to £5 a week, skilled workers up to twice that amount. My father always seemed to be working and I saw very little of him. He worked a three shift system, what we called days, afternoons and nights. The day shift from 7 am till 2 pm meant leaving home just after six, returning just before three in the afternoon. The afternoon shift was 2 till 10, the night shift 10 pm till 7 am. He worked almost every weekend as British Celanese was in continuous production which had been mainly switched over to war production such as parachutes, so that my impression in the war years was a man who was either just going to work or one who had just arrived home to have a meal and, if on night shift, to retire to bed. However he always seemed to find time for his gardening, an hour to study racing form and place a bet and ask me a few questions about school, always keen to know that I was pursuing my studies and doing homework. I usually managed to say something to keep him happy.

One moan he did have was that he was now paying income tax. Before the war he had paid little or none, now that he was working so many hours - something like 56 hours a week - he had become another taxpayer ('They stopped thirty bob this week'). Income tax had risen from the pre-war 5/6d (27p) in the £ to 7/6d (37p) in September 1939, 8/6d (42p) in July 1940 and finally reaching ten shillings (50p) in April 1941. By the end of the war, no less than 12.5 million were paying income tax compared to less than four million pre-war.

In 1940 a new method of collecting tax from weekly wage earners was introduced by which an amount was deducted from each wage packet based on estimated earnings over a period, rather than having to pay a lump sum at the end of the year and in 1943 a Pay As You Earn scheme based on current earnings was introduced which has lasted till this day.

More women were working including my mother who was doing canteen work and the family income had gone up considerably resulting in increased pocket money and something for national savings. I bought stamps at school, stuck them in a book and exchanged them for a certificate when I had collected fifteen shillings worth (75p) which promised to repay twenty shillings and sixpence (£1.02) in ten years. Savings stamps and certificates were popular Christmas and birthday presents, especially from aunts and uncles, which led to some disappointment: just when I had been expecting a chemistry set, a turntable for my Hornby train or the Magic Beano book, I was presented with five sixpenny savings stamps. It didn't seem the same.

The savings campaign had begun in the autumn of 1939 with posters proclaiming LEND TO DEFEND THE RIGHT TO BE FREE which was changed later to HIT BACK WITH NATIONAL SAVINGS. All kinds of promotions were used and I particularly remember a travelling cinema during the summer months. One Saturday in May 1940 it appeared on Ilkeston Market Place together with a large complement of the town council and officials including the Mayor, Mayoress, macebearer and all the regalia and trappings. While they sat on chairs at the front (armchairs for some of them) the townsfolk stood round in a semi-circle watching patriotic films.

During the school holidays in August the cinema appeared again, this time on Bennerley Avenue, much to our delight, when I went along with a few friends to watch films of our glorious fighting forces: guns of battleships pounding the enemy, Spitfires and Hurricanes shooting down Heinkels, Junkers and Dorniers by the dozen and our troops attacking enemy positions. The fact that our forces had retreated from France and Norway and the Battle of Britain was beginning did not seem important, it was all good patriotic stuff: we cheered in the right places and promised to buy national savings stamps.

A decorated single decker Midland General omnibus was driving round the town advertising the savings campaign in June 1940 with the slogan SAVE TO DEFEND and it was actually carrying passengers. I made several unsuccessful attempts to catch it but it always seemed to be going in the other direction. A huge sign in the shape of a Nazi jackboot greeted us as we entered the Market Place. It was affixed to the Town Hall and indicated the amount of savings raised and we checked the daily total on our way to school. Ilkeston's target for the year 1940 was £250,000 and this was passed with six weeks to spare.

However the big week was War Weapons Week. I had now finished the posters which had taken numerous sessions, having to clear away when the next meal was imminent or for some other activity which had priority. The posters were duly delivered to a beaming pair of ladies and within hours they were displayed in windows of shops and houses.

The main aim of the War Weapons Weeks which were held throughout the country was to re-equip the forces with tanks, guns and ammunition following the huge losses of equipment left behind at Dunkirk. Each town and village was given a target; Ilkeston's was £200,000, sufficient for twelve light tanks.

It was turned into a week of events, mainly organised by the town council. There were football matches on Manor Ground involving service teams, a boxing tournament and various other sports activities such as keep fit, while savings groups had people going from door to door selling stamps and certificates, in fact you couldn't go far without being made aware of it.

The big event of the week was a procession, said to be the largest since the pre-war carnivals. We remembered the carnival bands in their elaborate costumes headed by drum majors, the Ilson Middies, the Harmonicas, Ilkeston Gypsies, the Imperials and many others, parading and competing with partisan crowds cheering them on. Now the carnival bands had gone, victims of the war, but we had the military and their impressive bands playing There'll Always Be an England, Tipperary, and Run Rabbit Run.

People were standing shoulder to shoulder as the procession, headed by the Mayor and corporation proceeded down Bath Street to the Manor Ground where we witnessed marching displays and a musical programme. Ilkeston had not known such pomp for many a year and a great roar went up as a low-flying Spitfire dipped in salute.

When the final total was announced the following Saturday in the Market Place (£222,887, enough for fifteen light tanks) another great roar went up, Ilkeston had done it. All our half crowns and sixpences had achieved the target. However when the figures were released later it showed that about half the total was from large insurance companies and banks: £20,000 from the Pru, £11,500 from Britannic, £10,900 from Pearl, £10,000 each from the four banks in Ilkeston, £7,000 from the Co-op, £5,000 from Derby Savings Bank, £5,000 from the hosiery firm A. Booth and a massive £15,000 from Ilkeston Corporation. It all sounded rather stage managed.

Back to Cotmanhay where I had been keeping a close eye on the barometer gradually creeping up during the week. There was the final total, the red ink above the target figure showing £460. I rushed home to tell my parents. Cotmanhay had done its bit and raised more than expected to buy shells for our tanks to fire at the panzas.

I had been trying to keep up with my war diary but sometimes it lapsed for several days, then I had to go hunting for previous days' papers to catch up, not always possible as Dad had often lit the fire with them. However I was delighted to see the appearance of a series of paper back books of a daily war diary issued by Cherry Tree Books on behalf of the Sunday Times. The first was entitled 'The First Six Months' followed by 'The Second Six Months' and so on. I managed to collect the whole series of twelve books. As the foreword in one of the issues said 'It is a true diary: that it is written at the end of each day and is not altered afterwards.'

Writing the diary every day didn't always work out for me, especially if I had a lot of homework or there was a good film on at the pictures. There was also essential listening on the wireless, especially Tommy Handley's ITMA which everybody listened to. Wherever you went, people were repeating the catchphrases: 'Don't forget the diver', 'I go - I come back', 'Can I do you now sir?', 'Don't mind if I do' and so on. Other favourites were 'Big-hearted ' Arthur Askey and Richard 'Stinker' Murdoch in 'Band Waggon' and Harry Korris, Robby Vincent and Cecil Frederick ('Ramsbottom, Enoch and Me') in 'Happidrome.' Probably the outstanding comedian of the war was Robb Wilton who started his patter with 'The day war broke out ....' and then went on to describe his adventures as a Home Guard, firewatcher or special constable ('I ran like mad up the street, after all I didn't want to get blamed for it'). The BBC gave us something to laugh about.

Other popular programmes included Children's Hour with 'Uncle Mac' and 'Toytown', In Town Tonight, Monday Night at Eight, Worker's Playtime, Ack-Ack Beer-Beer, The Brains Trust, Appointment with Fear, Music Hall, Sandy's Half-hour and Hi Gang!

My diary was recording events in North Africa where German General Rommel had arrived in February 1941, pushing the British back to Tobruk. In June we were withdrawing our troops across the Western Desert back towards Egypt. European campaigns were also going badly for us. In March 1941 I had written 'British troops arrive in Greece.'

'A waste of time' said Uncle Billy. Our troops should be kept here, not fighting other countries' battles. We've only got the Home Guard and they're not much cop.' Uncle Billy was not enamoured of the Home Guard; he thought they were a lot of old men playing at soldiers.

His feelings about Greece proved correct when the following month Germany attacked Greece and Yugoslavia. 'Yugoslavia capitulates' I wrote on 17 April followed quickly be '22 April, British troops withdraw from Greece' and '23 April, Greek army surrenders to Germans.' As I looked at my map of Europe I could see that Germany had now conquered so many countries: Austria, Czechoslovakia, France, Holland, Belgium, Luxemburg, Denmark, Norway, half of Poland, now Greece and Yugoslavia, while Italy was allied to Germany. The swastika dominated the map.

There was little good news during the first half of 1941 but people seemed to be resigned to it, more preoccupied with rationing, shortages and the blackout. The feeling seemed to be that we would win in the end with Churchill as leader, in the meantime we would suffer and complain. Then in May we heard some good news which caused great excitement for a few days: we had cornered the German pocket battleship Bismarck which had caused our shipping so many problems. For months our navy had been giving chase, now with the help of Swordfish aircraft from the Ark Royal it had been caught and sunk. But almost at the same time we had more bad news, the sinking of our biggest battlecruiser, the Hood, in the same engagement. She sank within a matter of seconds with only three survivors out of a ship's complement of 1,421.

But the most astonishing news came on 22 June when Hitler invaded Russia. 'The Nazi hordes' as Churchill called them swept fifty miles into Russia in a well-planned operation on the first day, capturing ten thousand prisoners and destroying over a thousand Russian aircraft. This called for a Churchill speech to the nation. Although no supporter of the Communist regime, Churchill said: 'The cause of any Russian fighting for his hearth and home is the cause of free men and free peoples in every corner of the globe.'

When people got over the shock of the attack they were pleased that Hitler would have to divert much of his forces away from Britain and the general feeling seemed to be 'he's bitten more than he can chew', an expression I heard more than once, even though at first the Russians were in retreat after the surprise attack. Many people had a soft spot for Russia, but even those who disliked the Communists thought the news was good.

Newspapers and magazines were full of the news. I saw a copy of the magazine Illustrated with a long article entitled 'Hitler versus 180,000,000 Russians' which said 'This super nation which we British are wont to call just Russia, though she includes several European and many Oriental races, has swallowed up invaders before .... whatever his immediate successes there are too many Russians for Hitler.' There were pictures of marching troops ('11,000,000 soldiers'), parachutists jumping from planes ('30,000 planes and 100,000 paratroops'), tanks ('250,000 war machines'), Stalin ('man of steel') and other pictures showing the might of Russia. I copied the details in my war diary and stuck some home-made hammer and sickle flags on my wall map. It certainly made up for the bad news we had been getting.

People were beginning to feel a little more confident, especially as the bombing had stopped. Although the Government were still warning us to carry gas masks, few were doing so. The Ilkeston Advertiser conducted a small survey and although it covered only a short period of observation in the Market Place one late afternoon, the results were interesting. Out of 112 passers-by, only 17 carried gas masks and ten of these appeared to be returning from work where employers probably insisted on their staff carrying them.

Describing this as 'alarming' the Advertiser commented that 'Townspeople treat with disdain the repeated warnings by both Government and local ARP officials .... a number were carried about in battered cardboard boxes and in two instances the mask was actually protruding from the container.'

One of the 95 people without a mask was a member of the Council which urged people at all times to carry their masks. I think this showed that people believed the Nazi threat had receded considerably.

I was now in my last term at Hallcroft. I had been offered a free place at Ilkeston County Secondary School under the 'late transfer' system after I came top of the class in the Spring term of 1941. Examinations held no perils for me, it was just physical training and games lessons I tried to dodge, leading to the wry comment of my p.t. teacher in the end of term report, 'Does his best.'

The free place pleased my parents, especially Dad who regularly bought educational books for me, often 'Reader's Offers' from national newspapers. Dad had always done physical work and had no wish that I should follow in his footsteps. 'I want you to work with a pen, not a pick and shovel' was his advice and he helped me achieve it.

So I was fitted out with a new blazer and school cap and given an impressive brown leather school satchel on my birthday, 4 August. Life was to enter a new phase.